An **ICL** Christian Education/Christian School Resource

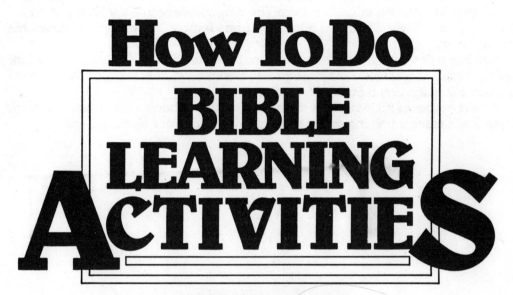

How To Do
BIBLE LEARNING ACTIVITIES

AGES 2-5

by Karen Klein · illustrated by Catherine Leary

GL International Center for Learning

INTERNATIONAL CENTER FOR LEARNING
A Subsidiary of GL Publications, Ventura, California, U.S.A.

About the Author

Karen Klein, is director of Indian Valley Nursery School in Souderton, Pennsylvania, and directs the children's summer ministries in her church. She has a B.S. degree in Christian education from The King's College in New York and an M.Ed. degree in Early Childhood Education from Temple University in Philadelphia, Pennsylvania.

She has a rich background of experience in education and Christian education, having served as a Director of Christian Education, an elementary school teacher and administrator, and a Sunday School teacher.

As a member of ICL's seminar teams for Sunday Schools and Christian schools, Karen leads teacher training seminars in many cities across North America.

Scripture quotations unless otherwise indicated, are from *The Authorized King James Version of the Bible*. Other versions quoted are: *TLB, The Living Bible*, Copyright © 1971 by Tyndale House Publishers, Wheaton, Illinois. Used by permission. *NIV, The New International Version*, Holy Bible. Copyright © 1978 by New York International Bible Society. Used by permission.

Published by International Center for Learning
GL Publications, Ventura, California 93003.
Printed in U.S.A.

ISBN 0-8307-0849-9

WHERE TO FIND. . .

3

BIBLE LEARNING THAT CHANGES LIVES

In early childhood Christian education, the role of learning activities has long been underestimated because it has not been fully understood. The focus of attention in teaching the Bible to young children has been the content—filled with plans for what the teacher is to do, and often containing only brief suggestions for what the children are to do (other than listen to the teacher). Bible lessons that contain aim-related learner-centered activities and experiences enable young children not only to understand and retain Bible truths, but also to respond with appropriate attitudes and actions. A fully effective ministry with young children, whether it be Sunday School, churchtime, or weekday preschool, needs to provide learner involvement through a wide variety of activities. It needs to meet the developmental needs of children under six.

When we begin to understand the nature of how young children think and learn, we become increasingly open to communicating God's truth through learner-centered activities. A child eagerly involved in using paint to make a vegetable print can be guided by a caring adult to think, talk and interact with others about God's provision for food, and respond with a thankful heart (attitude) to God in prayer for His love.

How do young children acquire information, understand it, and appropriate it in their daily experiences? Seldom does a child "learn" something without having acted on it, or participated in it mentally and physically. "Knowledge is constantly linked with actions or operations . . . its origin arises from interactions between subject and object," says the famous educator, Jean Piaget. For example, a child under six or seven cannot fully understand the term "fishing" unless he has actually experienced it. If he has seen a picture of someone fishing, or has seen someone fishing from a distance, he may have a limited idea of what it means to go fishing, and be able to repeat some information about fishing to you. However, this child knows nothing about how to operate a fishing line, what bait is like, and how it feels to have a "live one" tugging on the line. There is a big difference.

And so it is with learning Bible truths. We can talk about Jesus showing kindness to His disciples and then pray "help us all to be kind this week," hoping that the concept of kindness transfers into the child's everyday life. A better approach includes time for young children to work together in meaningful activities, guided by a teacher who labels and encourages acts of kindness as children interact with each other, and relates what the children are doing to what the Bible says about kindness. In this way, children are not only told about kindness, but they actually learn it through first-hand experiences right in the classroom! Bible learning activities play a significant part in meaningful Bible learning for young children. They are one way of making God's Word a part of the child's everyday experiences.

Perhaps you are asking, "If active learning is the key to effectiveness, then how can I plan and use Bible learning activities with my class?" The rest of this book will help you to do this.

Taking turns is a good way to be kind.

BIBLE LEARNING ACTIVITIES FOR YOUNG CHILDREN—How They Work

1. Bible learning activities are a portion of the total session planned for young children. In most cases they occur at the beginning of the session and vary in length (or time offered) according to the program. For Sunday School and Churchtime programs lasting one or one and a half hours each, the Bible learning activities segment lasts 20 minutes to 40 or 45 minutes. In a preschool weekday setting, learning activities (also called free choice time, centers, etc.) can last up to one and a half hours or more—sometimes half the total session.

Sample Sunday School Session

9:30-10:00 A.M.	Bible Learning Activities
10:00-10:10	Together Time
10:10-10:30	Story and Activity Page

Sample Preschool Session

9:00-10:15 A.M.	Free Choice Learning Activities
10:15-10:30	Group Time
10:30-10:45	Snack and Rest
10:45-11:15	Outdoor/Indoor Large Muscle Play
11:15-11:30	Story/Listening

2. The classroom is arranged with equipment and materials that enable children to choose freely from selected and planned activities. Not only do children choose, but they freely move from one activity to another during this time.

3. Three to five children can comfortably work at one time on a Bible learning activity. Limiting the number of children that can participate in an activity at one time helps foster good social relationships and allows the teacher to give individual guidance to this small group. Also, materials are more easily shared cooperatively with only four children participating at once in an activity. Limiting the number of children in a certain activity can be accomplished in several ways.

- Have only four chairs available (plus one for the teacher) as an automatic clue that up to four can work at once.
- In the block or music area, for example, post at the child's eye level a sign with the numeral "4". The teacher can assist children as they count out four participants.
- Comments such as this help: "We have four children working with blocks now, but when Jamie is finished in a few minutes, it will be your turn."

4. The number of Bible learning activities offered during a session depends on the needs of the children as well as the size of the class. In Sunday School and Churchtime, a class of 15 to 20 children should be offered four to six Bible learning activities. A smaller class of six or eight children would need at least two choices, with perhaps a third one for variety and interest. In a preschool weekday program, certain activities are a regular part of the school day. Examples of these basic choices might be block building and home living, as well as games and puzzles. Bible learning aims can be integrated in these daily activities through the teachers' use of guided conversation. Skilled teachers recognize that telling Bible stories is only part of good curriculum planning. Preschool programs should include a variety of aim-related Bible learning activities to support and extend the Bible lessons used

in the school. In this way children will understand and relate the Bible story and its concepts to their everyday experiences.

5. In a Sunday School setting it is important that each Bible learning activity is guided by a teacher. This can be done on a unit basis. For example: One teacher will plan and carry out a home living Bible learning activity for four weeks (or one unit of lessons), guiding children with comments and questions appropriate to the Bible aim. As each Bible learning activity is led by a teacher, children move freely from one area of the room to another, participating in or completing several activities during the session. Teachers are not just "watching" or "caring for" children while they "play," but rather acting as facilitators of the learning that is taking place during this valuable block of time. The teacher's role in Bible learning activities is to use conversation about the child's actions to guide the child's thoughts toward specific Bible aims.

In a preschool program, not all activities offered can be guided by a teacher (assistant teacher or classroom aide). However, certain activities can be planned daily which reflect Bible-related aims and include conversation, comments, and questions that encourage Bible learning. For example, during a unit about creation, a variety of general activities can be planned such as block building, puzzles, painting, and home living, while one or two Bible-related activities can be offered to help children focus their understanding on God's world and things that He made. These might include a flannelboard activity (using pictures or shapes of objects God made) and a God's Wonders table with plants, seeds and flowers as well as pictures of God's creation.

Bible learning activities provided both on Sunday and during weekday programs can greatly increase the child's ability to understand and use Bible content through the skillful guidance of a caring teacher.

Creating the Environment for Learning—Guided Conversation

Guided conversation is the key ingredient in making Bible learning activities effective teaching tools. The teacher's role in talking with children during an activity cannot be underestimated. Combining words with actions in a relaxed climate greatly increases a child's ability to respond to Bible truth. Through guided conversation you not only increase a child's knowledge and understanding, but also help him build positive attitudes about himself, about others, and about church and school.

In communicating with children, you convey ideas through your actions as well as your words. In fact non-verbal messages are more powerful, many times, than verbal messages. As you seek to create a learning environment where children are guided in everyday experiences toward spiritual truths, there are a number of communication skills which will help you to be successful in your efforts.

1. Use a natural tone of voice. Don't talk down to children. Avoid sugary sweet words.
2. Give direct eye contact when speaking to a child. Bend down or sit down if necessary to show the child you are focusing on him.
3. Use the child's name often.
4. Non-verbal signals of touch and smile are very important.
5. Actively listen to what a child is saying. You can accomplish this by repeating the child's words back to him, or by asking a question about what the child said to encourage further conversation.

6. Use your example, or model, to create understanding. Children will do what they see you doing. An example combined with an explanation is strikingly effective in influencing both understanding and attitudes.
7. Accept a child's feelings and ideas.
   - Support and encourage the process rather than the product.
   - Affirm a child's happy feelings as well as negative feelings during an activity. ("You really don't like working with finger paint, do you? You might want to play with the blocks, or read a book.")
   - Value children's work and effort whether or not the work is done correctly or completed to perfection.
   - Avoid correcting a child's mistake or wrong answer. Either find some element that is correct to affirm, or ask the child questions that will help him think through what he has done or said.
8. Use praise and encouragement to motivate a child toward success. Positive comments about specific efforts and actions encourage children to want to do the right thing. Focusing on a child's strengths and assets builds strong feelings of acceptance and self-worth. Children are naturally eager to please; they thrive on being noticed in positive ways.
9. Keep your Bible-related aim in mind as you talk to children about what they are doing. Encourage children to talk about what they are doing and thinking. Help them assist and support one another.
10. Help children make choices and decisions. However, don't offer a choice when there really isn't one. "It's time to put our blocks away" is more useful than "Would you like to put blocks away now?" Even better is "It's time to clean up our room. Would you like to put away blocks, or help wash out paint brushes?"

Keep in mind that guided conversation during a learning activity usually takes practice before it begins to feel natural. If you use these guidelines, your Bible learning activities will soon come alive for children as you informally direct children's thoughts to the Bible truth you want them to learn. No longer will learning activities seem like projects, or just play times, but times of valuable and enriching Bible learning.

BIBLE LEARNING ACTIVITIES—OR CRAFTS?

The following list will help you determine whether an activity is a **craft** (focusing on the **product**) or a Bible learning activity (focusing on the **process**). Of course, there are times when Bible learning activities have some characteristics of crafts and vice versa).

Bible Learning Activity

Children create, discover, explore, question and respond.

Teacher talks *with* children. Children talk and interact with one another.

Focus is on the process.

Teacher conversation and encouragement is a key factor in learning (associating activity with Bible truth).

A Bible learning activity is an important part of the session; it occurs before the Bible story to prepare children for Bible content (readiness).

Several activities are offered at once—all planned to accomplish one aim. The learner chooses one activity.

Small groups of three or four children work with one activity; children are free to move from activity to activity throughout the time block.

Craft

Children follow predetermined pattern or directions.

Teacher often talks *to* or *at* children.

Focus is on the product.

Completing the project is the key factor.

A craft usually follows the Bible story as a way of illustrating the Bible truth.

Usually only one project is offered.

Children all work on the same project at the same time.

WORKING WITH A SLOWER/ DISABLED LEARNER

In order to guide a slower or disabled learner in profitable Bible study, it's important to identify some of his/her characteristics and then to discover and use methods that take into account these characteristics. Become familiar with the general characteristics listed here, but be aware of the fact that not all of these characteristics will apply to all children who have learning difficulties. Adapt the suggested tips to meet the needs of *your* learners.

Some characteristics a slower/disabled learner may demonstrate:
1. Unusually short attention span—learner does not complete task;
2. Easily distracted:
   - out of seat frequently;
   - distracted by outside noises (e.g., people out in hall);
   - seeks attention (unusually aggressive to other children or unusually withdrawn);
3. Short-term auditory or visual memory (e.g., can't recall specific facts);
4. Poor muscle coordination;
5. Poor verbal communication skills;
6. Very easily frustrated—gives up easily;
7. Works carelessly and too fast;
8. Learning problems can show up in many areas: language development, pre-reading skills, writing tasks.

Some tips for working with a slower/disabled learner:
1. If you notice a learning problem, discuss it with the child's parents.
2. Discuss with the child's other teachers (e.g., school teacher, Sunday School teacher) effective ways of working with the child.
3. Use methods/materials that motivate and interest the child:
   - multi-sensory materials—felt boards, 3-D aids, touch-and-feel items, dolls dressed like Bible characters, story cards, items to smell, puppets;
   - hand movements that reinforce concepts—up/down, in/out, right/left, top/bottom.
4. At monthly planning/training meetings, devise an individualized plan for the extra-slow learner, making sure goals are realistic for him/her.
5. Speak clearly, distinctly, not too fast. Give one direction at a time.
6. Use animated voice, with expression—avoid monotone.
7. Use direct eye contact and appropriate facial expressions.
8. Be close enough to touch child when attention wanders.
9. Recapture attention by saying child's name or asking child's opinion.
10. Use repetition in order to strengthen short-term memory.
11. Express the same idea in different words, from simple to more complex.
12. Be sure to use very literal terms—not abstract.
13. Avoid over-stimulation that is caused by giving too much at once.
14. Choose Bible learning activities that help strengthen eye-hand coordination: lacing, matching, stringing.

15. Keep unneeded materials out of the child's reach.
16. Provide structured environment (clearly-defined schedule, rules, procedures).

WORKING WITH AN ADVANCED/ GIFTED LEARNER

Even though a list of general characteristics will not apply to all advanced/gifted learners, it's helpful to be familiar with some characteristics that are typically common to these children. Use and adapt the suggested tips to meet the needs of *your* learners.

Some characteristics an advanced/gifted learner may demonstrate:

1. Exceptional verbal communication skills;
2. Highly motivated; completes his/her tasks;
3. Needs a variety of experiences;
   - intellectual—reading;
   - creativity—art, music;
4. Physically larger—appears older than his/her age group;
5. Doesn't need much guidance;
6. Has leadership ability.

Some tips for working with an advanced/gifted child:

1. Provide additional visual aids, perhaps from curriculum materials of older children.
2. Provide activities using tape recorder, teaching records, filmstrip.
3. Involve the child in learning about life in Bible times; e.g., he/she can:
   - make items such as scrolls or a Bible time village;
   - roleplay life in Bible times.
4. Give a complete set of directions (instead of one instruction at a time).
5. Give extra assignments that make use of child's special gifts/abilities (planning some part of the lesson; finding and sharing information needed in the lesson, helping a slower learner).
6. Always have extra Bible learning activities/games ready. An advanced/gifted child completes more, faster than other children do.

Age-Level Symbol Used in This Book

Each Bible learning activity has a symbol that indicates the approximate age level(s) for which that activity is most appropriate (adapt according to the needs/ abilities of *your* learners). The darkest area indicates the most appropriate age(s); the lighter shading indicates an additional range of appropriateness.

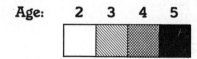

RESOURCES
For General Supplies

(including puzzles, blocks, rhythm instruments, etc.):

Beckley-Cardy
1900 N. Narragassett Ave.
Chicago, IL 60639
(313) 622-5420

Childcraft
20 Kilmer Road
Edison, NJ 08818
(201) 572-6100

Children's Book and Music Center
2500 Santa Monica Blvd.
Santa Monica, CA 90404
(213) 829-0215

Kaplan Corporation
600 Jonestown Road
Winston-Salem, NC 27103
(919) 768-4450

Lakeshore Curriculum Materials Co.
2695 E. Dominguez St.
Carson, CA 90749
(213) 537-8600

Moyer/The Teacher's Store
25 Milvan Drive
Weston, Ontario M9L 1Z1
(416) 749-2222

The Judy Company (puzzles)
4325 Hiawatha Ave. So.
Minneapolis, MN 55406
(612) 721-5761

Ward Music, Ltd.
412 W. Hastings St.
Vancouver, BC V6B 1L3
(604) 682-5288

For Child-Size Furnishings

Childcraft
20 Kilmer Road
Edison, NJ 08818
(201) 572-6100

Community Playthings
Rt. 213
Rifton, NY 12471
(914) 658-3141

For Audiovisual Equipment

A.F. Milliron Co., Inc.
366 Coral Circle
El Segundo, CA 90245
(213) 640-0600

AGS Visual Craft
4820 W. 128th Place
Alsip, IL 60658
(312) 385-1919

I-MED (Instructional Materials
    and Equipment Distributors)
1520 Cotner Ave.
Los Angeles, CA 90025
(213) 879-0377

Scholar's Choice
777 Douro St.
Stratford, Ontario N5A 6T9
(800) 265-8541 or 265-8550
(audiovisual equipment and
school supplies)

Wholesale Educational Suppliers Co.
63 S. 4th Ave.
Mount Vernon, NY 10550
(800) 243-2518

Teacher's Resource Materials

Barber, Bill. *Discipline and the Young Child.* Ventura, CA: GL Publications, 1977.

Foster, Donna. *Building a Child's Self-Esteem.* Ventura, CA: GL Publications, 1977.

Haas, Carolyn Buhai. *The Big Book of Recipes for Fun.* Northfield, IL: CBH Publishing, Inc. 1980.

Harrell, Donna and Haystead, Wesley. *Creative Bible Learning for Young Children.* Ventura, CA: GL Publications, 1977.

Hohmann, Mary; Banet, Bernard; Weikart, David. *Young Children in Action.* Ypsilanti, MI: High/Scope Press, 1979.

Iverson, Rachel. *Talking Together with Young Children.* Ventura, CA: GL Publications, 1978.

Rottman, Fran. *Easy-to-Make Puppets and How to Use Them, Early Childhood.* Ventura, CA: Regal Books, 1978.

Self, Margaret, ed. *Little Ones Sing.* Ventura, CA: Praise Book, 1972.

Bible Learning Activities—Early Childhood (filmstrip/cassette). Ventura, CA: ICL (GL Publications), 1982.

Songs for 2's and 3's (cassette tape). Ventura, CA: GL Publications, 1979.

Songs for 4's and 5's (cassette tape). Ventura, CA: GL Publications, 1979.

ART ACTIVITIES

Of all the Bible learning activities available, those related to art are perhaps the most enjoyable and stimulating to the young child, offering a wide range of possibilities for creative expression.

Art activities offer children relaxed opportunities to explore and use materials to express not only ideas, but also feelings. For example, a shy, timid child may express himself/herself with only a few strokes of a brush, while an angry child may show his/her emotion by pounding, squeezing and twisting clay.

As in most areas of a young child's growth, artistic expression follows a developmental pattern. Children under two or three begin to explore art materials, manipulating them to discover what happens. Strokes and movements are often uncontrolled. Expressions at this stage should not be labeled "just scribbling," but should be viewed as an important step toward developing control and appropriate use of materials. Young children progress to the next stage where their art work is under control. The child knows what the materials will do and has a definite, though often changing, purpose in mind. Then the child becomes capable of actually expressing and representing certain ideas.

The teacher's role is clearly to encourage the child's efforts in each stage of development, focusing on the process of the art experience, not the finished product. The emphasis in Bible learning activities is on providing enjoyable and meaningful art experiences for children to do, rather than beautiful and clever art objects for them to make. As teacher and child work together, opportunities for natural conversation provide teachable moments for children to learn important scriptural truths.

Here are some general guidelines to follow when using art Bible learning activities:

1. Plan ahead for the activity by actually trying it out yourself. You will be more at ease and able to focus on the child's thoughts and ideas if the procedure is familiar to you. Practicing it ahead also helps avoid potential problems as you think about adapting the activity to your particular children.

2. Provide enough materials for three or four children to work comfortably without having to wait long periods of time for a turn. For example: Have available two or three glue brushes, four pair of scissors and five or six clay tools. Also provide extra sheets of paper (paper bags, plates, etc.) for those children who need to try again, or perhaps want to try something twice (if there is time).

3. Always write the child's first name on any art work so it can be identified easily. Lower case letters should be used, except for first letter of the name which should be a capital. (Allow the child to do this whenever possible, even if all the child can do is write the first letter.)

4. Use conversation to support and encourage the child's efforts in his Bible learning activity. Don't insist on perfection or correctness from an adult perspective. Avoid "improving" or "finishing" a picture for a child.

5. Involve children in being responsible for materials. Encourage them to do things for themselves. For example, children can open glue bottles, use a stapler and wash brushes. When an activity is finished, involve children in specific cleanup tasks such as putting away materials and sweeping the floor.

6. All art materials require proper storage. Plastic containers (margarine cups or bowls with lids, ice cream tubs, etc.) are ideal for clay and play dough storage. Small jars are great for tempera paint and glue. When using tempera with children, shallow aluminum pie, cake and roll pans are excellent. So are muffin tins and plastic bowls.

Cutting Tips

Cutting with scissors takes a great deal of finger coordination and control and this task can be frustrating to the young learner. Much practice is needed for success. Provide child-size scissors with blunt tips; make sure that left-handed children are provided with scissors marked "lefty." A child needs to be guided in placing his thumb and middle finger in the holes and shown how to open and close the scissors so they will cut. (Training scissors are available from school supply houses. They have extra holes so the teacher can assist.)

Begin cutting experiences by drawing straight, short, heavy lines with dark crayon. You may need to hold the paper stiff as the child attempts to cut. The child may need help in learning how to hold and turn the paper as skill in cutting increases. When the child is able to cut straight lines easily, slanted lines, then curved lines and finally, simple figures, provide new challenges.

Folding Tips

When children are just learning to fold paper, hold the edges together and let the children do the creasing.

Painting Tips

1. Liquid tempera is the most convenient to use. Powdered tempera must be mixed vigorously, but is less costly. Good quality paint can be made using liquid starch. Just add powdered tempera or a few drops of food coloring to the starch and mix together. When children are just learning to paint, begin with one color. Then expand the number of colors.
2. Fill containers and pans only as deep as the bristles (or enough to cover bottom of sponge or gadget) to limit spills. Keep adding paint as needed.
3. Brushes with long handles and wide, stiff bristles are best for young artists. Use a separate brush (gadget, sponge, etc.) for each color paint offered.
4. Spread a vinyl tablecloth on the floor when painting on an easel.
5. No sink nearby? Use a dishpan or bucket half-filled with soapy water for quick cleanup. Place dishpan on a small chair or low table and have paper towels and sponges handy.
6. Have smocks ready for use to protect clothing from misguided strokes of paint. Men's short-sleeved shirts worn backwards and clipped with a clothespin provide easy, comfortable protection. Since only a few children participate at once in an art activity, only about four or five smocks are needed.

7. Show child how to rest brush on side of jar to remove excess paint.
8. Show child how to wipe up drips.
9. Allow children's paintings to dry in a safe place away from traffic areas. Use twine or fishnet to make a clothesline where pictures can be hung with clip clothespins. A clothes drying rack is a good addition where space allows. Or place painting on the floor along the wall.
10. Clean brushes with soap and cold water and store, bristles up, in a coffee can or wrapped in newspapers.

Tips for Using Clay and Play Dough

1. Have a variety of tools available—enough for three or four children to work together. Store clay in airtight containers when not in use. Homemade play dough may last a month or two. After that, it should be replaced.
2. Dried clay or play dough objects can be painted with tempera paint. When dry, brush with clear nail polish to preserve color if desired.
3. Adding a few drops of food coloring or tempera when mixing play dough, as well as a few drops of lemon oil, peppermint or cinnamon flavoring provides more sensory enjoyment.

RECIPES FOR ART MATERIALS

SALT-FLOUR DOUGH

Children enjoy the relaxation and unending variety of forms that come with molding, squeezing, rolling and pounding dough. This activity becomes even more fun when the children mix the dough themselves. Try these no-cook recipes (recipes 1-3) for different textures.

Recipe No. 1

    2 parts flour
    1 part salt
    1 tablespoon (15 ml) alum

Add water and dry tempera to achieve desired consistency and color.

Recipe No. 2

    4 cups (1 l) flour
    2 cups (.5 l) salt
        food coloring
    ¼ cup (.06 l) salad oil
    ⅛ cup (.03 l) soap flakes
    2 cups (.5 l) water
    ⅛ cup (.03 l) alum

Recipe No. 3

    1½ cups (.375 l) flour
    1 cup (.25 l) cornstarch
    1 cup (.25 l) salt
    1 cup (.25 l) warm water

Recipe No. 4 (cooked)

    1 cup (.25 l) flour
    1 cup (.25 l) water and food coloring
    ½ cup (.125 l) salt
    1 tablespoon (15 ml) cooking oil
    2 teaspoons (10 ml) cream of tartar

Cook until consistency of mashed potatoes. Do not boil. Knead until cool.

With all recipes, if dough is sticky, dust with flour. If dough is stiff, add water. All recipes need to be stored in airtight containers. Recipe No. 3 hardens nicely and can be painted if sculptures are to be preserved.

PEANUT BUTTER CLAY

    Peanut butter
    Dry, powdered milk
    Honey

Mix equal parts peanut butter and powdered milk. Slowly add honey to achieve desired thickness. If mixture is too sticky, add more milk.

Mold the "clay" into any desired shape. For added fun, decorate with seeds and raisins. Then, eat it!

HOMEMADE PAINT

    ½ cup (.125 l) vinegar
    ½ cup (.125 l) cornstarch
    Food coloring

Mix vinegar and cornstarch together. Add food coloring slowly as you stir, until desired color is reached. If paint is too thin, add cornstarch. Add vinegar if too thick.

FINGER PAINT

    Liquid starch
    Soap flakes
    Powdered tempera

Mix equal parts of starch and soap. Add tempera to achieve color desired. Add more starch if too thick, more soap if too thin.

FINGER WHIP

    Soap flakes
    Water
    Beater

Mix equal parts water and soap flakes. Whip with beater. Add more water to thin, more soap to thicken.

PUD

    ½ box cornstarch
    Water

Pour cornstarch onto shallow cookie tray. Add water slowly and stir. Pick it up. Squeeze it. Watch what happens!

BASIC FURNISHINGS AND EQUIPMENT FOR ART ACTIVITIES

Furniture

For 2s-5s
Painting easel (2-sided)
Table
- 30x48-inch (75x120 cm) surface, or round with 40-inch (100 cm) diameter
- For 2s and 3s—20 inches (50 cm) high
- For 4s and 5s—22 inches (55 cm) high

4-6 chairs
- For 2's and 3's—10 inches (25 cm) high
- For 4's and 5's—12 inches (30 cm) high

Small clothes drying rack (for wet paintings)
Open shelves with closed back—12 inches (30 cm) deep

Equipment and Materials

For 2s-5s
Long-handled paintbrushes—3/4-inch (1.9 cm) bristles
Paste
Large newsprint sheets
Salt/flour dough (see recipes on page 21) or Play-Doh
Tempera, assorted colors
Smocks or aprons
Large crayons
Sponges

Additional Materials for 4s and 5s
White glue, glue sticks
Construction paper
Large sheets manila paper
Scissors (blunt tip)
Clay

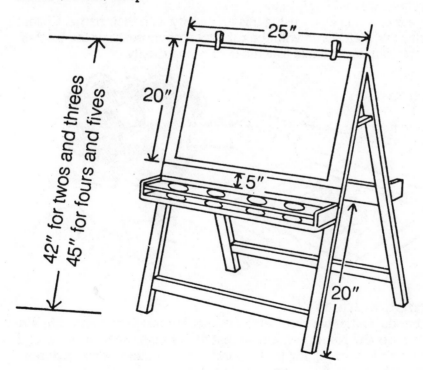

42" for twos and threes
45" for fours and fives

25"

20"

5"

20"

5 in. = 12.5 cm.
20 in. = 50 cm.
25 in. = 62.5 cm.
42 in. = 105 cm.
45 in. = 112.5 cm.

23

SAND PICTURES

See explanation on page 13.

Purpose: That children use sand to express or represent an idea.

Materials
☐ Lid of a shirt box or rectangular tray
☐ Sand
☐ Rubber cement with brush applicator
☐ Construction paper—any size smaller than the lid or tray

Procedure
1. Children use the rubber cement, brushing strokes on their paper. It may be necessary to do just a portion of the picture at one time and repeat the process because of the quick-drying nature of rubber cement.
2. Before the rubber cement dries, children place their paper in the box lid or tray and gently drizzle sand over the paper, covering the strokes made with the rubber cement.
3. Children then carefully lift the paper and allow excess sand to fall back into the lid or tray. Sand should adhere well to the rubber cement and when dry, children will have a textured picture to look at AND feel. Note: Check with the custodian before using sand indoors.

Variations
1. Salt works equally as well with this activity.
2. Four- and five-year-olds will enjoy using this art activity with their name. Children can write the letters of their name with the rubber cement brush, or the teacher may assist the children not yet able to write their name clearly.

Guided Conversation Ideas
"God gives us hands so that we can feel things that are rough and smooth. What is something that is smooth? Name something that feels rough. Feel this sand and tell me something about it. We're going to use sand today to make some pictures that we can not only look at but that we can feel as well."

CRAYON RESIST

Purpose: That children paint over crayon pictures to express their ideas and feelings.

Materials
☐ White or manila construction paper—9x12 inches (22.5x30cm)
☐ Crayons
☐ Tempera paint (one color)
☐ Tempera brush
☐ Shallow pan for paint

Procedure
1. Children use crayons to draw on the paper, guided by the teacher's conversation. For example: Children may be guided to draw something for which they are thankful—"It is a good thing to give thanks" Psalm 92:1. Or, children may draw themselves—"I am . . . wonderfully made" Psalm 139:14; "God created man (people)" Genesis 1:27.
2. When children complete their work with crayons, they are then ready to use the paint. Children use a brush to paint over their crayon picture with large, even strokes until the whole paper is covered with paint. The crayon should "resist" the paint, creating an interesting effect.

Variations

1. Using this activity with two- and three-year-olds, the teacher may want to prepare simple crayon drawings ahead and have the children paint over them. For a theme about God giving food for all, draw simple pictures of fruits and vegetables. A simple heart with the words "God is Love" inside provides the opportunity to talk about this Bible thought as the child is painting.
2. Play a mystery game with this activity. Four- and five-year-olds will enjoy guessing things God made as they paint over crayon drawings that have been prepared ahead by the teacher with *white crayon* or *wax candles*.

Guided Conversation Ideas

Use this suggested conversation when reinforcing the aim, "I am . . . wonderfully made" Psalm 139:14. Have ready pictures of children and children's faces. "What do you see in these pictures? The children look happy. What are they doing? Touch the boy who is running. Look carefully at the girl's face in this picture. Touch her nose. What else do you see about her face? Name some other things God gave to us on our faces. You can use these crayons and paint to tell something about yourself. God gave you a face with eyes, nose, and a mouth. God made you with dark hair and soft skin. Use these crayons to draw something about yourself. Would you like to draw just your face or your whole body? Whatever you choose to do is fine. I like the circle you have made with the green crayon. That looks like it might be the outline of your face. I'm glad God made you with a face that can smile. And I'm glad that God gave you hands that can do good work."

MELTED CRAYON PRINTS

Purpose: That children make prints using grated crayons and wax paper, helping them appreciate God's gift of color.

Materials:
- ☐ Grated crayon pieces—all colors
- ☐ Wax paper—cut in 10- or 12-inch (25 or 30cm) lengths
- ☐ Newspapers or several sheets of newsprint
- ☐ Iron
- ☐ Cellophane tape
- ☐ Optional: fall leaves or dried flowers and weeds

Procedure
1. Pad the table with newspapers or sheets of newsprint.
2. Children sprinkle grated crayon pieces on one sheet of wax paper.
3. If desired, children may add fall leaves or dried flowers.
4. Then children place a second sheet of wax paper over the first. Cover with a sheet of paper and iron with a warm iron. Crayon pieces should melt and form a pleasing, colorful design.
5. Crayon prints may then be taped to a window, allowing the children to see the sunlight shine through the colors.

Guided Conversation Ideas
"We're going to discover some things about God's gift of color, using these crayon pieces." In assisting children to be successful in the tasks required for this activity, try this: "I'll put my hand over your hand on the iron and we can press together." Guide children to talk about what they have done and to respond in their awareness of colors. "What happened to the crayon pieces after we ironed them? What colors do you see now? Let's tape our print to the window so the sun can shine through the colors."

FUN WITH WOOD

Purpose: That children use wood, nails and string to make a design or pattern.

Materials
☐ Scrap wood pieces (soft pine is best, 5"x7" or 8"x10"—12.5x17.5 or 20x25 cm)
☐ Nails with large heads
☐ Hammer
☐ Sandpaper
☐ Yarn or string

Procedure
1. Children sand the wood to be sure there are no rough edges.
2. Children pound 8 or 10 nails into wood in a random pattern.
3. Then they use string or yarn to wind in and out of the nails to create a pattern.
NOTE: Young children enjoy working with wood. However, close teacher supervision is needed.

Variations
1. Children can use rubber bands instead of yarn or string to stretch over the nails in a variety of patterns.
2. Children may also want to nail together several scraps of wood to make an object or a shape.

Guided Conversation Ideas
"We have some nails and a hammer to use with this wood today. We're going to carefully hammer the nails to the wood like this (demonstrate). Then we can use this yarn to weave in and out of the nails." Encourage good use of materials with comments like, "I like the way you are carefully holding the nail with your thumb and finger." For those having difficulty say, "You hold the nail like this and I'll hammer."

CLAY

Purpose: That children use clay to express their creativity and to shape and form objects representing their ideas.

Materials
- ☐ Enough clay for three or four children (see recipe on pages 21, 22)
- ☐ Plastic container with lid (for storage)
- ☐ Various tools—wooden cylinder (rolling pin), cookie cutters, plastic knives, bottle caps, etc.

Procedure
1. Sitting at child-size tables, children use clay to shape, pound, press and roll, with the help of the tools available.
2. Younger children will simply enjoy the process of working with clay, while fours and fives may use the clay to represent ideas and objects relating to the Bible aim. For example: Children use the clay to shape a well that helps them focus on events in the story of Rebekah, or to make a Bible-time house that helps them recall how Jesus healed the man let down through the roof.

Guided Conversation Ideas
"I can see that you are enjoying your work today with our clay. Your hands can make it roll into the shape of a ball. I'm glad we can use clay today."

"We're going to use this clay today to help us think about Rebekah and how she was a kind helper. What did Rebekah do that was kind? Where did she get the water for the thirsty man? In Bible times there were no drinking fountains. People had to get their water from a well. What do you think a well looks like? Let's use our clay to work on shaping a well like the one Rebekah used."

PICTURE MURAL

Purpose: That children place selected pictures on a large sheet of paper to depict a Bible theme or accomplish a Bible learning aim.

Materials

☐ Pictures cut from magazines, calendars, catalogs and greeting cards. For example, a unit on thanking God might include the following selected pictures: moms and dads, trees, flowers, food, homes, churches, animals and children.
☐ Shelf paper or extra-large sheet of paper (any kind)
☐ Glue or paste

Procedure

1. Children choose from the pictures provided those items they wish to depict on their mural.
2. They glue these pictures to the large sheet of paper.
3. Older children may want to print their names near the pictures they have contributed to the mural. Teachers can letter the names of younger children.

Variations

1. More mature fours and fives may want to cut out their own pictures from magazines and catalogs.
2. A mural makes an excellent bulletin board! Make sure that it is placed at the children's eye level so that small eyes can see it.

Guided Conversation Ideas

"What are some times you say thank you? What has God given you that you can thank Him for? Tell me something you see that you are thankful for. Why are you thankful for trees?"

Simple statements by the teacher during this activity model a thankful attitude; for example, "Thank you, God, for Mommies. Thank you, God, for my friend Jimmy."

TABLETOP MODEL

Purpose: That children construct and display items representing a selected Bible story or theme, enabling children to recall and understand Bible content related to that story or theme.

Materials
☐ Construction paper
☐ Chenille stems (pipe cleaners)
☐ Clay
☐ Toothpicks
☐ Optional items: cardboard pieces, tissue paper, paint, crayons, smooth stones, bits of sponge, twigs
☐ Glue, tape, etc.

Procedure
1. Children select something related to a Bible aim that they wish to construct or design from the materials provided. For example, in making a tabletop model of creation the children might choose items such as animals, trees, plants, sun, water, etc.
2. Children work with the materials—cutting, shaping and putting together items that will make up the display. The teacher may have to guide certain parts of this procedure, such as helping a child put his tree in some clay so it will stand up.
3. The teacher provides the base and background for the display, and carefully guides the children as they prepare and put their items in place.
4. The model can be displayed in the classroom, hallway, foyer or library.

Variations

1. A model of a Bible-time house helps children understand how Bible people lived. Include some people figures for the children to move and play with as you talk about certain Bible people who might have lived in a house like this.
2. During the Christmas season, a model or display of the nativity, using wood or other unbreakable figures helps children to remember why we celebrate Christmas and to think about the important events that happened at the time of Christ's birth.

Guided Conversation Ideas

How a child first approaches a Bible learning activity is very important. A teacher's words of encouragement and help can make a big difference in a child's feelings and efforts during the activity. "Good morning, Josh. We have some papers and clay here that we are using to make things that will show what God created when He made our world. Tell me one thing you know God made. What else did He create? What materials would you like to start with in making a _____? Your work reminds me of how great God is to be able to make our world. No one but God could create our world."

Then, as the child progresses in his work, use specific comments such as "I can tell you like the color blue. You seem to be working hard on those branches. I'm glad you're making a tree for our display." Conversation relating to the Bible content can be used as the children observe and touch their work. "I see some birds and a few animals." "God made all animals and everything that flies." "Touch what God made that swims." "We're glad that we could work together on this model so we can see all the wonderful things God has made."

SEWING CARDS

Purpose: That children use yarn to sew a pattern on a flat board or Styrofoam tray to reinforce a Bible thought.

Materials
☐ Styrofoam meat trays (or cardboard approximately 5x7 inches (12.5x17.5 cm)
☐ Yarn—lengths of 20-30 inches (50-75 cm)
☐ Cellophane tape
NOTE: Determine design or pattern desired and use a pencil or a nail to punch holes in the tray or cardboard to make the pattern. (A hole punch works well with cardboard.) Two- and three-year-olds may simply enjoy sewing (using four or five punched-out holes) with no Bible pattern, whereas fours and fives may be able to transfer ideas about a boat, star, Bible, etc., to conversation about Bible events.

Procedure
1. Prepare yarn ahead by knotting one end and wrapping cellophane tape around the other end to make a tip.
2. Children use the lengths of yarn to sew on the prepared trays and/or cards.

Variation
Sewing cards can also be used effectively to add to, or complete, a picture drawn on cardboard or a tray. Example: Yarn is used only on the water or the sun's rays.

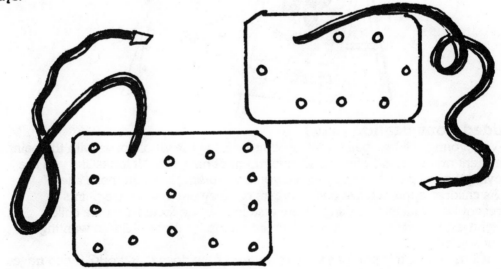

Guided Conversation Ideas
"You're doing a good job of using your fingers to sew on these cards. I'm glad God gave you fingers so you can try new things in school/church. If you let your yarn come up through this hole, you might notice something that will remind you of our Bible story. Your sewing card reminds me of how God cared for Moses."

BRUSH PAINTING

Purpose: That children express their thoughts, feelings, and ideas through painting.

Materials
- ☐ Tempera paint (liquid or powdered mixed to creamy consistency)
- ☐ Baby food jars, other small containers to hold paint
- ☐ Large, long-handled brushes
- ☐ Easel or tabletop covered with newspapers
- ☐ Smocks or old shirts turned backwards
- ☐ Sponge (for easy cleanup of drips and spills)
- ☐ Large sheets of newsprint 12x18 or 18x24 inches (30x45 or 45x60 cm)
- ☐ Water for cleanup (plastic dishpan works well if no sink is nearby)
- ☐ Clothesline, drying rack or other device on which to dry paintings

Procedure
1. Children put on a smock before painting to protect their clothing.
2. Children use the brush to paint on the paper provided. Two- and three-year-olds will enjoy working with one color at a time. Fours and fives can handle several colors at once, but remember, a separate brush and jar are needed for each color used.

Guided Conversation Ideas
Very young children paint, making lines or filling the whole page with the paint. Comment on the child's efforts and enjoyment of his work. "It looks like you are enjoying the red paint today. I can see you are working hard on those lines."

As children approach five and six years old they are able to use paints to represent actual ideas and things. Conversation can be focused on the child's thoughts and expressions of a Bible-related theme for those children wanting to "paint something."

"Tell me about this part of your picture. And how does that work? (Encourages further thought.) Your Dad has a smile, I see. I'm glad God gave us dads."

Children who choose to paint something not related to a Bible thought or concept can be encouraged in their enjoyment of the activity and appropriate use of the materials. For example: "I like how your hands can use that brush. I see you are painting yellow over the blue strokes you've already made. I'm glad you can paint with your friends today."

IMPRINTS

Purpose: That children discover how God made them special by using their fingers to make an imprint.

Materials
☐ Ink pad (rubber stamp pad)
☐ Cloth and cleaning agent (for cleaning fingers)
☐ Paper for imprint
☐ Marking pens

Procedure
1. Children press their finger or thumb onto the ink pad and then press their finger or thumb to the paper.
2. Children may want to repeat this process several times, noticing the many lines and shapes their fingerprint makes. Child's name should be printed on his/her fingerprint paper.

Variations
1. Children may want to make pussy willow fingerprint pictures, using a paper where several branch-like strokes have been made with a marking pen. Children add fingerprints up and down the branches.
2. Older fours and fives would have fun adding "faces" to their fingerprints, using thin line marking pens.

Guided Conversation Ideas
"The ink made a print of your finger, Peter," or just, "That's your fingerprint, Peter." "Look at the lines and shapes your fingerprint made!" "God made everyone's fingers to look different." "Only you have those special lines and shapes." Susan's lines in her fingerprint are special, too." "Thank you, God, for our fingers." "I like the way you used the cloth to wipe the ink from your fingers."

CRAYON RUBBINGS

Purpose: That children use crayons rubbed on paper to extend a Bible thought or idea.

Materials
For a leaf-rubbing picture
☐ White paper 8½x11 inches (21.5x27.5 cm)
☐ A variety of leaves
☐ Crayons—with the paper peeled off

Procedure
1. Children choose a leaf or leaves and place flat on table.
2. Children then cover the leaves with a piece of paper.
3. With the crayon held the long way, they rub the crayon back and forth across the paper until the shape of the leaves shows clearly on the paper.
4. Care must be taken not to move the leaves or paper while working. Teacher may need to help with this.
5. A clear print of the leaves underneath should result with interesting patterns of veins.

Variations
Other interesting textures appear when children use rubber mats, tree bark and carpet pieces with this crayon activity.

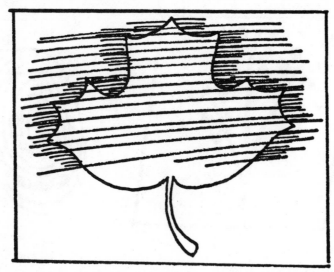

Guided Conversation Ideas
"What have you noticed is happening to the trees outside?"
"It is fall and the leaves are coming off the trees."
"God planned for trees to lose their leaves in the fall. It gives us a chance to see them up close." "Tell me about other changes in the fall."

PAPER BAG PUPPETS

Purpose: That children make puppets and use them to represent and express Bible thoughts and concepts.

Materials
☐ Paper bags—lunch size
☐ Crayons and/or marking pens
☐ Construction paper, fabric, trims (scrap pieces work well)
☐ Yarn (cut in small pieces)
☐ Scissors
☐ Glue

Procedure
1. Children take a paper bag and turn it so the folded part is facing them.
2. Children choose pieces of construction paper or yarn and use them as parts of the face—eyes, nose, mouth. Children glue the pieces to appropriate places on the paper bag. Yarn can be used in a variety of ways and is especially fun to use as hair. Use fabric and trims for clothing.
3. When children finish gluing and drawing their puppet face—and perhaps a body, too—they will want to use their puppet to talk and express ideas as the teacher guides the conversation.

Guided Conversation Ideas
"You're making your puppet with a smile. I can tell your puppet is going to say kind things." To help the child anticipate the use of his puppet, you might say something like, "As you work with that crayon, Mark, think of some things you might want your puppet to say when you are finished making it." Or, "It looks like your puppet is almost ready to say something."

You may want to encourage the children to name their puppets and make up short stories about them as they focus on living a Bible truth such as being kind. "What kind thing can your puppet do now to help the hurt boy?"

STRING PAINTING

Purpose: That children enjoy expressing their ideas and thoughts, using string and paint.

Materials
- ☐ String—cut in 10- to 15-inch (25-37.5 cm) lengths
- ☐ Construction paper or other art paper—12x18 inches (30x45 cm)
- ☐ Tempera paint
- ☐ Shallow pan—one for each color offered
- ☐ Newspaper or large sheets of newsprint
- ☐ Smocks (to protect clothing if needed)

Procedure
1. Children hold one end of the string and dip it into a shallow pan containing a small amount of tempera paint.
2. Children hold string up over pan while excess paint drips off the string.
3. Then children move the string across the paper, creating shapes and patterns.
4. When children have finished using the string to "paint," they return it to the shallow pan. They need to be careful to leave several inches free from paint as they place the string over the edge of the pan.
5. Several colors may be used, if desired, as the children repeat this process.

Variation
Place paint-covered string in desired pattern on the bottom half of the paper. Carefully fold paper in half and press so string design is printed on both halves of the paper.

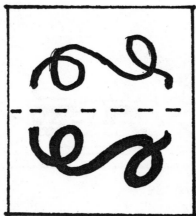

Guided Conversation Ideas
"I see you have used the string to make an interesting pattern on your paper. Your hands can do many wonderful things. I'm glad I can be your friend and work with you today. I'm glad God has given me friends. Thank you for sharing the blue string with Adam. Adam is a good friend, too."

FINGER PAINTING

Purpose: That children use their fingers, hands and paint to express their ideas and feelings.

Materials
☐ Powdered or liquid tempera paint
☐ Liquid starch
☐ Finger paint paper (with glazed surface) or shelf paper
☐ Newsprint or newspapers to cover table

Procedure
1. Mix liquid starch with tempera ahead of time. Or pour one or two tablespoons of liquid starch onto the paper and sprinkle some tempera over it.
2. Children use their hands to spread the mixture over the paper, making designs and patterns with fingers and hands.
3. Encourage the children to spread and smooth the mixture across the paper and to work with this activity as long as they desire.

Variation
Paint on table or tray; then press paper on design. Remove paper and let it dry.

Guided Conversation Ideas
"I like the way you are using your hands to make some curvy lines. Your hands can make many different designs. I'm glad God gave you hands to do good things." "It looks like you're ready to wash your hands. Thanks for finger painting with us today."

Four- and five-year-olds can be guided to represent ideas that reinforce a Bible story. For example, "Let's think about the time Jesus calmed the storm as we make some waves on our paper with blue paint. Jesus' friends were afraid when the storm came." Or, "I like the way you made a green tree with the finger paint. It reminds me of things God has made."

SEED COLLAGE

Purpose: That children use seeds to make a design which helps them focus on how and why God gives us seeds.

Materials
☐ Seeds of all shapes and sizes; dried pods, weeds and flower parts also work well
☐ Stiff, heavy paper such as oak tag or cardboard—5x8 or 8x10 inches (12.5x20 or 20x25 cm)
☐ Rubber cement or glue
☐ Brush for glue or rubber cement
☐ Optional: Clear contact paper to cover completed picture to keep seeds securely on paper

Procedure
1. A wide variety of seeds and other dried items should be placed in a shallow box so children can easily choose the items they want to use in their design.
2. Children brush rubber cement or glue on a small section of their paper and then arrange seeds and other items on it. Making the design in sections prevents the glue from drying before the child has finished applying the seeds.

Note: This activity is not appropriate for children under three.

Variations
1. Children may glue seeds to a paper plate.
2. Use a paper punch to make two holes in the completed picture; add yarn, and picture is ready for hanging.
3. Seeds may also be used to add interest, meaning and texture to other art activities. For example, seeds may be added to pictures of growing plants or gardens as children focus on the spring season.

Guided Conversation Ideas
   "Why does God give us seeds?" "What happens to seeds when you plant them?" "Let's find the seeds in this apple." "Who made the seeds?" Guide children in singing "God Made Everything" (page 11 of *Little Ones Sing,* listed on page 15 of this book).

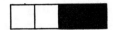

FINGER PUPPETS

Purpose: That children create finger puppets that will encourage them to think and talk about a Bible story, Bible-related concept or life application story.

Materials
- ☐ Construction paper of various colors
- ☐ Patterns or shapes for desired figures (for example, butterfly, boy, girl, angel, Bible characters)
- ☐ 2- or 3-inch (5 or 7.5 cm) squares of construction paper for securing puppets to fingers
- ☐ Cellophane tape or glue

Procedure
1. For younger children not yet able to cut, have 2- or 3-inch (5 or 7.5 cm) shapes cut out ahead. Older children will enjoy cutting their own shapes that have been traced on construction paper.
2. Assist children in taping the shape to the middle of the square. Roll the square to fit the child's finger and tape securely.
3. Children talk and move the puppets as teacher guides the conversation.

roll paper square

tape in back

Variations

1. Children may want to use crayons to add some interest to their finger puppet. Example: "You're giving your boy puppet brown hair, I see."
2. A wide range of materials can be chosen to make this activity creative and interesting for young children. Try using fabric, wallpaper, foil, or stiff oak tag.

Guided Conversation Ideas

"It pleases me to see you working quietly making finger puppets." "Tell me what shape you have chosen." "Thank you for sharing the tape with Peter." "I'm glad you came to church/school today."

"See how your fingers can move the butterfly?" "I'm glad God gave us butterflies."

A life application gives opportunities to talk about everyday experiences that please the Lord. For example, "Tell me what kind words your girl puppet will say to show love to her friend." "What good thing will your puppet do today?" "Our Bible says, 'Be kind to each other'."

ART ACTIVITIES

STRAW AND TOOTHPICK CONSTRUCTIONS

Purpose: That the child experience the enjoyment of constructing shapes and designs which may illustrate or represent a Bible truth.

Materials
☐ Toothpicks
☐ Straws
☐ Bits of Styrofoam, Play Doh or marshmallows
☐ Glue or paste

Procedure
1. Children make a design of their choice by joining straws or toothpicks together with Styrofoam, Play Doh or marshmallows. A small box or Styrofoam block works well as a base.
2. Teachers may want to encourage children to design and construct a certain shape such as a boat or a house in order to stimulate conversation about a Bible concept or story.

Variations
1. Children may glue flat toothpicks or straw pieces to paper either as a collage or in a design or shape. Consider using crayons or paint to add color.
2. Shapes may be made from toothpicks or straws glued or tied together and attached to a string for hanging as a decoration (examples—stars, boats, kites).

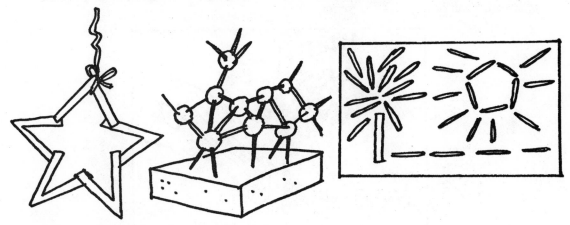

Guided Conversation Ideas
Encourage the children by offering specific, positive comments about what they are doing. "I like the way you used your fingers to put the straws together." "I see you worked hard gluing those pieces to the paper." "That star you are making reminds me of the stars that God made in the sky." "Thank you, God, for stars that shine at night."

ART ACTIVITIES

SPONGE PAINTING

Purpose: That children enjoy working creatively with materials, together with other children, while at church/school.

Materials
☐ Tempera paint (powdered or liquid)
☐ Sheets of construction paper (light colors with dark paint; dark colors with light paint)
☐ Sponges cut in small 2-inch (5 cm) pieces (cut when damp or wet)
☐ Spring-type clothespins
☐ Newspapers or large sheets of newsprint to cover the table (if needed)
☐ Shallow containers (aluminum pie pans or trays work well and are disposable)

Procedure
1. A separate shallow pan and sponge clipped to clothespin will be needed for each color tempera that is used. One color is suggested for very young children, while two or three may be offered for experienced painters.
2. Pour just a small amount of tempera into shallow pan.
3. Children should handle sponge by the clothespin, dipping the sponge into the paint and dabbing it on the paper.
4. Children can be encouraged to rub, spread, press, or just paint with the sponge to make a design of their choosing.

Variations
Children might enjoy focusing on how God gives us snow by sponge painting with white paint on dark blue paper.

Guided Conversation Ideas
"We're glad you can make a sponge painting today." "I can see you worked hard on your design." "I like the color you chose." "I can tell you enjoyed your work." "Thank you for sharing the red sponge with Matthew. It pleases God when you share."

HANDPRINTS

Purpose: That children discover how God made them special, as they use their hand to make a plaster of paris imprint.

Materials
☐ Plaster of paris (a five-pound box is plenty for 10-12 children)
☐ Large pot
☐ Heavy spoon for mixing
☐ Water
☐ Stiff paper plate—dessert size
☐ Paper punch
☐ Rickrack or yarn
☐ Sink or dishpan nearby for cleanup

Procedure
1. When all materials and children are ready, teacher should mix just enough plaster of paris to work with—three children at a time—following directions on package label. (Mixture will harden too soon if too much is prepared at one time.)
2. Teacher then pours enough mixture into a stiff paper plate, leaving an edge (rim) of the plate showing.
3. Immediately, child places hand (guided by teacher) on the wet plaster. Child presses just enough to make a well-outlined print of the hand.
4. Cleanup should follow as soon as possible.
5. When the handprint is set, child punches two holes in the edge of the plate (at the top of the hand). He/she strings rickrack or yarn though the holes so the handprint can be hung.
6. Because of the quick-setting nature of plaster, more than one teacher may be needed to assist with this activity.

Variation
Child may paint around handprint.

Guided Conversation Ideas
Use conversation that focuses children's thoughts on God's gift of hands. "How many fingers do you see? Thank you, God, for giving us hands. Why are you happy God gave you hands?"

Since this activity involves a long-lasting product, children may benefit from conversation about their hands for weeks as both teachers and parents talk with children about God's gift of hands.

GADGET PRINTING/PAINTING

Purpose: Children use paint and gadgets to print patterns and designs for wrapping paper or greeting cards.

Materials
- ☐ Tempera paint (liquid, or powdered mixed with liquid starch or detergent)
- ☐ Shallow pans, jar lids or muffin tin
- ☐ Paper to print on (shelf paper, construction paper, etc.)
- ☐ Newspapers or large sheets of newsprint to cover tables
- ☐ Paper towels
- ☐ Gadgets—corks, spools, lids, hair curlers, corn cobs, kitchen utensils

Procedure
1. Pour a small amount of tempera paint into the shallow pan or other container.
2. Children dip gadget into the paint and blot it on a paper towel. Then they press it down on the paper (once or several times) as long as the print shows.
3. Children repeat this process, printing a pattern in a repeating design. They can use one gadget with one color paint or several gadgets with one or more colors of paint.
4. If making greeting cards, children may want to fold the paper and write their names on the inside. Teacher may assist in writing names for younger children. Through conversation and questions, you can guide the children to think and talk about those who will receive the cards. Record on the card the children's words of kindness and caring, such as, "I hope you get well soon" or "I hope this card makes you happy."

Variation
An equally enjoyable and effective alternate to this activity is the use of cut-up vegetables and fruit to print. We suggest trying carrots, potatoes, onions, apples, and oranges.

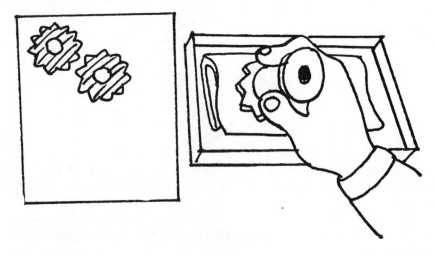

Guided Conversation Ideas

"I'm glad we can use paint and these gadgets to make get-well cards today. Have you ever been sick? How did you feel? Did you receive a special card when you were sick? How did it make you feel when you got a card in the mail? God cares about us when we are sick. When we send a get-well card, it shows our friends that we care about them. Who are some sick people you know? How would Mrs. Smith feel if the mailman brought her a card from you?"

As children work, these comments would encourage them in their efforts: "I like the pattern you are making. Your hands are doing good things. You really enjoy painting, don't you? What are some kind words you want to say to Mrs. Smith to help her feel happy? Tell me some other words I can write in your card."

TISSUE PICTURES

Purpose: That children design or construct a picture representing a flower (forsythia) or other work of creation.

Materials
☐ Yellow tissue paper cut into small 1- to 2-inch (2.5 to 5 cm) squares
☐ Glue—small amount in shallow pan or dish
☐ White construction paper—9x12 inches (22.5x30 cm)
☐ Marking pens or crayons
☐ Forsythia cuttings

Procedure
1. Prepared ahead—long lines for stems or branches drawn on construction paper. Older fours and fives may draw their own branches.
2. After observing and talking about forsythia, children crumple lightly a piece of tissue paper and dip a small part of it into the glue.
3. Children then place the tissue piece on the paper by a branch. This process is repeated until the branches are blooming!

Variations

1. Using green and/or fall-colored tissue paper, children dab tissue leaves onto tree shapes (trunk, branches) drawn ahead by the teacher.
2. Bright, spring-colored tissue pieces can be glued onto a butterfly shape 4 to 6 inches (10 to 15 cm) high. This activity works well using slightly stiffer or heavier paper. The butterfly can be finished off by making a small fold across the body and placing a round-head clothespin through the middle (between the wings). A pipe cleaner makes a great antenna.

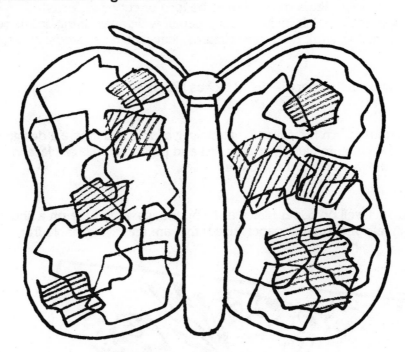

Guided Conversation Ideas

Have available live cuttings of forsythia, or a real butterfly in a plastic jar or box for children to see and touch. If the "real thing" is not available, have a picture at eye level so children can be stimulated to talk and think about flowers, butterflies, or other things God created.

"What is this we have on the table today, Susan?" or "What do you see in this picture?" "Tell me something you notice about this flower." "Good thinking, Susan. You noticed that the little flowers are yellow. Let's see what Matthew can tell us about these flowers." "Where would you see flowers like this?" "Tell us how we get flowers." "Yes, God gives us many kinds of beautiful flowers." "We're going to use tissue paper and glue to make something that will remind us of the flowers God gives to us. This flower is called a forsythia." "Matthew, you can give Susan a paper and I'll help you pick out some tissue pieces to get started."

Continue to guide children as they work, encouraging them in their efforts. "Susan, you did a nice job on that branch. Now you can put a few flowers over here on this other branch." "Thanks, Matthew for wiping the glue that spilled on the table. That was a kind thing to do."

COLLAGE

Purpose: That children express ideas creatively, using a variety of materials glued to a paper.

Materials
☐ Construction paper pieces (pre-cut or to be torn or cut by children)
☐ Other suggested materials include tissue paper, wallpaper, string, fabric scraps, foil, cardboard and yarn, magazine pictures, leaves, beans, seeds, sticks, flower petals
☐ Glue
☐ Sheets of construction paper—9x12 inches (22.5x30 cm)

Procedure
Children choose from the collage materials available and create a design on their paper. It may be better to glue the paper first and press the collage piece in place rather than gluing the small collage piece.

Variations
Collage works well on paper plates and paper bags. If you are on a shoestring budget, try sheets of computer paper (used) that are readily available from many companies.

Guided Conversation Ideas
Encourage the cooperative use of materials and the enjoyment of being at church/school. "I like the way you have placed your pieces all in a row" or "You must like yellow, Scott; your design makes me think of warm sunshine." "Thank you for helping to pick up the scraps." "I see you are making flowers for your collage, Tommy. I'm glad God gives us flowers."

BLOW PAINTING

Purpose: That the child participate in an art activity which will result in a pleasing design that can be used for book covers or simple gifts given as an expression of love and caring.

Materials
- ☐ White or pastel-colored drawing or construction paper
- ☐ Squeeze bottle with tempera paint (liquid or powdered mixed with liquid detergent)
- ☐ Plastic or paper drinking straws
- ☐ Newsprint or old newspapers to cover table
- ☐ Water, paper towels, and sponges for cleanup

Procedure
1. Cover table with newspapers.
2. Place drawing or construction paper on the newspapers.
3. Squeeze little pools of paint on the paper. A small amount of paint is sufficient.
4. Point one end of the straw in the direction you want the paint to move.
5. BLOW! The straw should not touch the paint.

Variations
1. Use more than one color paint. As the colors meet and mix and form new colors, the child will enjoy talking about the newly-formed color.
2. If younger children are blowing, use food coloring. If blowing becomes sucking, the food coloring is a pleasant alternative to paint.
3. The designs may be used as backing for paintings, bookmarks for gifts, or book covers.

Guided Conversation Ideas
The blowing action will encourage children to explore ideas concerning God's wind. "How do you think the wind felt during the storm? How was it different from a gently blowing wind? Let's look outside. We cannot see the wind. What can you see that tells you the wind is moving? Listen to the wind. Tell about what you hear." "How has God used colors to create a beautiful world?" Look or walk outside. Locate colors that are blended as the blown colors blended.

GOD'S WONDERS

Bible learning activities that center around the wonders of God's creation are excellent tools for developing and enhancing spiritual truth in young children. Carefully chosen items displayed for children to touch, smell, taste, feel, and see give children opportunities to understand and be aware of God and His world. God's wonders displays that are continually changed with the seasons or focus of study allow teachers to guide a child's thoughts toward Bible concepts. Guided conversation can not only focus a child's attention on things that God has made, but also help a child respond in thankfulness to God for His great love toward us.

Many of God's wonders are not activities like art and drama, but are simply displays of things God has created that children can explore with their senses. Three types of materials belong in the God's wonders area:

1. Items and objects relating to a theme or unit of study (Examples: plants, shells, feathers).
2. Pictures or simple books to further extend a child's understanding of the objects displayed. These can portray the habitat or environment of the items displayed, for example.
3. Supplementary materials such as a magnifying glass, plastic containers, or watering can, which help clarify and extend a child's understanding of the items displayed.
4. The greatest wonders of all are the marvelous senses God has provided each child to see, touch, taste, hear and smell. Any materials which call on the child to use one or more of these senses are appropriate to include in this center.

The child's natural interest and curiosity in the world around him/her provides unlimited opportunities for teachers to involve children in Bible learning activities centered around God's wonders. Here are some examples of God's wonders activities/displays.

Leaves, twigs, dried flowers	Honeycomb
Fall weeds and seeds	Wasps nest (vacated)
Evergreens, holly, pine cones	Plants, flowers
Magnets, balance scales	Tulip and other flower bulbs
Chrysalis (caterpillar/butterfly)	Feathers, birds' nests
Shells, starfish, etc.	Eggs (hen, goose, peacock, etc.)
Rocks, sand, stones	Moss, pond plants
Seeds, soil	Antlers, fur, other animal skin
Pussy willows, forsythia buds	Insects
Animals	Vegetables and fruits
Sounds	
Textures	
Smells	
Colors	

BASIC FURNISHINGS AND EQUIPMENT FOR GOD'S WONDERS ACTIVITIES

Furniture
Low, open shelves with closed back—
12 inches (30 cm) deep

Equipment and Materials
Bible with pictures
Nature materials (see list above)
Magnifying glass

MAGNETS

Purpose: That children discover how God uses magnets to attract things made of iron or steel.

Materials
☐ Horseshoe magnet and/or bar magnet
☐ Objects such as:

paper clip	cotton ball
coin	cork
nail	wooden clothespin
plastic spoon	bottle cap

☐ Two shallow boxes or containers—one marked "Yes" and one marked "No"
☐ Picture of an electron magnet at work or children working with magnets. Also a simple picture book about magnets would work well displayed by the magnets.

Procedure
1. Children use magnet to touch each object, seeing if it is attracted to the magnet.
2. Those objects picked up by the magnet can be placed in the container marked "Yes", and those objects not picked up by the magnet can be placed in the "No" container.
3. Children take turns discovering which objects are attracted to the magnet.

Variations
1. Children will also enjoy experimenting with magnets and iron filings. Try placing the iron filings on the top of a hard plastic or acrylic board and use the magnet underneath the board to make the filings move around.
2. Children may discover ways to make use of small magnets throughout the classroom. Magnets can hold teaching pictures on a metal cabinet, for example.

Guided Conversation Ideas
"God made magnets so they pull and even pick up some things. Let's see what happens when we hold the magnet near this paper clip. Try the magnet near the clothespin. What happens? We have two boxes that we'll use to put these objects in when we decide which ones the magnets pick up and which ones it doesn't pick up. Let's put the paper clip in the container marked 'Yes'. This picture shows a big magnet that people use to do hard work. (Or, this picture shows some children using magnets to do some interesting things. Tell me what you see.) I'm thankful that God gives us magnets."

GROWING CARROT TOPS

Purpose: That children discover how carrot tops will sprout when placed in water.

Materials
- ☐ Carrots
- ☐ Small jar or other container—one for each carrot top
- ☐ Round toothpicks—three per carrot
- ☐ Water in pitcher or watering can
- ☐ Table knife
- ☐ Paper towels (for spills and drips)

Procedure
1. Children are guided to cut tops from carrots, with about one inch (2.5 cm) left on the top.
2. Place three toothpicks around the sides of the carrot, near the top. Do this with each carrot top you want to plant.
3. Children then fill their jars with water, placing carrot top so just the bottom is covered with water. Carrot top is secured in place by the toothpicks.
4. Check often to make sure the bottom of the carrot top is covered with water.
5. Soon green stems and leaves will begin to blossom on the carrot top.

Note: Children will surely enjoy having carrot sticks as a snack when doing this activity.

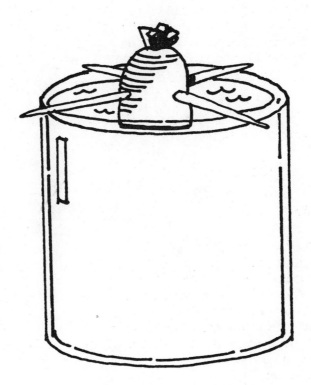

Variations

1. Children may enjoy watching roots appear when plant cuttings are placed in a clear jar of water. Swedish ivy and other common house plants work well.
2. In the spring it is fun to observe a dormant branch of shrubbery such as forsythia or pussy willow as it is brought inside and placed in water. Soon buds and other green signs of life will appear.

Guided Conversation Ideas

"Look closely at the top part of these carrots. What do you see? We'd like to help these carrot tops grow. What will we need to do? Yes, the carrot tops will need water to grow. When have you eaten carrots at home? How do they taste? Where does this orange part of the carrot grow? (Underground—it's a root.) The top part of carrots have green leaves and stems, but they've been cut off. Let's work together to put these carrots in water so we can watch what happens. We'll need these toothpicks to help hold our carrot tops up in the water. I'll hold the carrot top and you push the toothpick into the side right here. Good work, now let's try one more here and another over here."

GROWING THINGS/POTATO PLANT

Purpose: That children plant a potato to increase their awareness of God's plan for growing things.

Materials
☐ Baking potato with "eyes"
☐ Clay pot or other container for planting
☐ Small stones
☐ Potting soil
☐ Water

Procedure
1. Children place stones in the bottom of the pot (for drainage) and fill with potting soil.
2. Children either plant the whole potato or cut off a portion with an "eye" and just plant that piece in the soil.
3. Water the soil and place the pot in a sunny spot.
4. Within a few weeks children will notice shoots and leaves pushing through the soil.
5. When the leaves turn yellow, children should dig up the potato and see what has happened. Roots should have several tiny new potatoes.

NOTE: Children would enjoy having cooked or fried potatoes for a snack during this activity.

Variations

Children enjoy planting a wide range of things representing God's creation. Try building a young child's awareness of God's plan for growing things using these other ideas:

1. Plant miniature marigold seeds in a Styrofoam cup filled with potting soil (punch a hole in bottom of cup for drainage). If seeds are planted in March or early April, children will have a Mother's Day flower to take home.
2. Fours and fives can plant tulip, daffodil or crocus bulbs in the outside shrubbery beds of your church/school during the fall. How delighted they are when spring arrives and their plantings peak through the ground.
3. A sweet potato placed in a jar of water, tip down, will sprout a vine in several weeks. (Use toothpicks to suspend the potato in the jar.)
4. Plant beans, radishes, etc.

Guided Conversation Ideas

"Let's pass the potato around so everyone can touch it. What's happening to this potato? (It's getting eyes.) These white, pointy things are part of God's plan for the potato. Thanks, Jeff, for arranging the stones in the bottom of the pot. Now let's take turns adding some soil. Gary, you go first. We will have to wait several weeks to see what will happen. What do you think we will see first? Where can we place the pot so it will grow best?"

GROWING GRASS

Purpose: That children understand God uses water to make seeds grow.

Materials
☐ Small food tray for each child (foil, Styrofoam, plastic)
☐ Grass seed
☐ Paper towels
☐ Small pitcher or watering can filled with water
☐ Plastic wrap

Procedure
1. Children watch as teacher demonstrates pouring a small amount of water on a paper towel folded inside of a food/meat tray.
2. Children then fold a towel and place it inside a meat tray of their own.
3. Children pour a very small amount of water on their tray until the towel is saturated.
4. Now we are ready to sprinkle grass seed on the wet towel. Teacher assists in covering and surrounding the tray with plastic wrap to retain moisture.
5. Children are encouraged to take their trays home and watch as the seeds sprout within several days.

Variations
1. Plant seeds on a wet sponge or inside a plastic bag with a wet paper towel enclosed. Bag can be fastened to bulletin board where all can watch the seed's progress.
2. Use other seeds, such as radish or bean (green, lima, kidney) seeds.

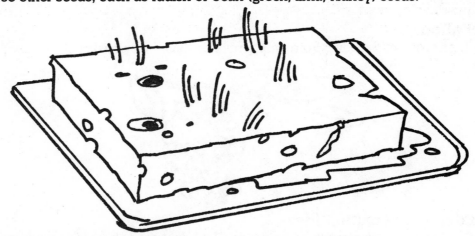

Guided Conversation Ideas
"I'm glad God gives us seeds so grass and other plants can grow. Tell me one thing seeds need in order to grow (water, sunshine, soil, etc.). What else needs water in order to grow? What would happen to our seeds today if we did not have water? How do most seeds get water to grow? Yes, God sends the rain."

PINECONE BIRD FEEDERS

Purpose: That children discover ways to care about things God has made.

Materials
☐ Pinecones—one for each child
☐ Thin wire, cut in 8- to 10-inch (20 to 25 cm) lengths
☐ Solid vegetable shortening (Crisco) or peanut butter
☐ Bird seed placed in shallow pan or tray
☐ Table knives
☐ Plastic sandwich bags or wax paper bags
☐ Optional: pictures of birds and bird feeders

Procedure
☐ Children wrap a piece of wire around the top of the pinecone so it can be hung from a tree branch.
2. Using table knives, children spread enough vegetable shortening or peanut butter on the pinecone to make the whole pinecone "sticky."
3. Grasping the wire and top portion of the pinecone, children roll it in the pan of bird seed. Seeds should cling easily to the shortening or peanut butter.
4. Carefully place the finished bird feeder in a plastic bag for protection. It is now ready to be transported to children's backyards or nearby trees where it can be hung (by the wire) from a low branch.
5. Children will receive a lot of enjoyment watching their feathered friends come for lunch!
Note: Soft cleanup cloths or a nearby sink with soap and water helps with the greasy hands.

Variations
Try making bird feeders from empty milk cartons, berry baskets, and scooped-out grapefruit rings.

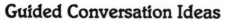

Guided Conversation Ideas
"God cares about everything He made. How does God show His care for you when you are cold and hungry?" "What are some things God gives you to keep you warm? Who helps you when you're hungry?" etc.

"God cares about the birds. What's one way God helps birds? How can we show that we care about birds?"

"I'm thankful that God cares about me and I'm thankful for the birds, too."

ANIMALS IN A JAR

Purpose: That children extend their awareness and understanding of God's plan for animals by observing and caring for animals in a jar.

Materials
☐ One gallon-size wide-mouth jar (available from restaurants)
☐ Nylon net (to cover top of jar)
☐ Pond water
☐ Pond plants, stones, soil
☐ Animal: choose from pond snail, water bug, tadpole, newt (salamander), or whatever can be collected

Procedure
1. Teacher and/or children collect animal from a local pond, stream, or lake, along with pond water and some surrounding soil and pond plants. Use plastic bags to collect animals and plants.
2. Arrange the soil and pond plants at the bottom of the jar. Fill jar half or three-quarters full with pond water.
3. Now the animal can be placed in the jar—his new home for a few weeks.
4. Place the netting over the mouth of the jar and secure with a rubber band.

Notes on care and feeding:
Snails: If you have two or three fresh-water plants extra food is not necessary.
Tadpole: Water plants will do. Do not leave jar in direct sunlight. Return tadpole to pond after a few weeks.
Newts: Canned dog food works well for food.
Waterbugs: They need small insects to eat.

Variations

1. Try collecting toads, earthworms, butterflies and moths to provide children with additional experiences with small animals.
2. Fish and hermit crabs are available at local pet stores and provide interesting conversation about God's wonders.

Specific instructions for this activity can be found in the following softbound book: *Pets in a Jar: Collecting and Caring for Small Wild Animals,* by Seymour Simon, Penguin Books, New York, N.Y. 10022.

Guided Conversation Ideas

"Tell me what you see in the jar. Yes, it looks like a shell, but can you see that it's moving? God made snails with a special shell covering. What else do you notice about our snail? God made snails with feet that aren't at all like ours. What can snails do that we can't do? What other animals could we find in a pond? God made all the animals that live in a pond."

DISCOVERING WITH OUR SENSES

Purpose: That children (1) increase their awareness of their sense of seeing, touching, smelling and tasting and (2) discover some qualities of fruit.

Materials
- ☐ Banana
- ☐ Orange
- ☐ Lemon
- ☐ Brown bag or cloth sack
- ☐ Knife
- ☐ Napkins

Procedure/Conversation
1. Teacher places fruit into bag beforehand.
2. Children guess what might be in the bag without touching it. "I've brought a bag to class today and there are some things inside. Without touching the bag, use your eyes and think about what might be inside. Teddy, what do you think is inside my bag? Why do you think that?"
3. Allow children to look, then reach inside and identify the object. "Let's use our hands now to discover what's inside. Aren't you glad God made us with hands so we can touch things? What do your fingers feel, Marsha? Tell us what it's like. What shape do you feel? Is it hard or soft?"

NOTE: Some children may be fearful of putting their hand in the bag until they see what is in the bag. Allow child to look and then reach inside and identify object.

4. Children can then remove the fruit to handle it, discovering more about the items through more skillful conversation. "God gives us eyes so we can see all things. What is it like not to be able to see? God knows we need our eyes so we don't have to guess about things. Tell me what your eyes see, Barry. Let's thank God for our eyes. Thank you, God, for my eyes."

5. As teacher cuts the fruit one at a time, children get to smell next. "What else has God given us that helps us discover about things? Let me give you a clue. We use this when we are in the kitchen or in a flower garden. Show me you know by wiggling what God gave you that you use to smell things. What do you smell, Marsha?"

6. Finally, cut fruit into small pieces, inviting children to taste. "The orange is sweet, but the lemon is. . .? How is the banana different from the orange? Thank you, God, for helping us enjoy food by giving us a tongue to taste."

Variations

1. Place pieces of cotton saturated with selected smells into small baby food jars or margarine cups. Let children guess what each smell is.
2. Fresh flowers (with a fragrance) displayed in a God's Wonders area or on a low table give casual opportunities for teachers to talk about God's gift of smell.
3. Activities and games focused on a child's ability to see various things lends itself to a greater awareness of God's gift of sight.
4. Any collection of familiar objects can be put into a bag for children to identify.
5. Put each object in a different sock. Children can feel socks, then reach inside to try to identify objects.

NATURE WALK

Purpose: That children discover the beauty and orderliness of God's world and His care for the things He has made.

Materials
☐ Containers for any specimens children find on their walk.
☐ A "walking rope" to keep children together (a length of rope with knots tied 2 feet (60 cm) apart, that children hold onto as they walk).

Procedure
1. Before taking the walk, talk with children about (a) what to look for; (b) safety rules such as all staying together, holding onto the rope, etc.; (c) other rules such as picking up things already on the ground—not leaves, flowers, and grasses that are still growing.
2. As you walk, talk about things you see. Avoid hurrying children.
3. Stop for a closer look at flowers, an insect or a rock.

Guided Conversation Ideas
Relate what children see to the beauty and orderliness of God's world and His care for the things He has made. "God planned for many trees to lose their leaves in the fall. In the spring the trees will grow new leaves."

MUSIC ACTIVITIES

Rhythm and song come naturally to children as an expression of their ideas and feelings. Some children sing loud, clear, and long with little encouragement, while others simply listen and tap their fingers, reluctant to make any audible response.

From the age of about eighteen months through the end of the fifth year, children's musical ability changes as dramatically as any other area of their life. No matter where children are in their expression and ability in music, it is an enjoyable and effective teaching tool which can easily be used in small group Bible learning activities to reinforce and support spiritual truth.

Music is an ideal way to help children learn and recall Bible content. Singing "Happy Easter, we will say, our Lord Jesus lives today!" helps children know an important Bible truth. In addition, music provides a way for children to express feelings and offer praise to the Lord. A song about prayer, for example, helps build attitudes of worship and respect for God. And music offers children opportunities to participate together actively in response to Bible truth.

While it certainly does help to be able to carry a tune, being a musician is not a requirement for using music with children. The relaxed, spontaneous, joyful attitude of a teacher is by far more important than correct pitch or elaborate accompaniment. Children respond beautifully to a warm, enthusiastic voice guiding them in listening to, and singing, meaningful and enjoyable songs.

In addition to using music as a Bible learning activity in itself, music can also be used to support and increase the effectiveness of other types of Bible learning activities. For example, sing "Who made the leaves? God did . . ." (number 11 in *Little Ones Sing*, listed on page 15 of this book) as you guide children in making leaf rubbings (see page 36) or as children look at leaves through a magnifying glass in the God's Wonders area.

When using Bible learning activities related to music, keep the following guidelines in mind.

1. Choose appropriate songs (see page 69).
2. Use visuals and objects to increase understanding of the song and create additional interest.
3. A child under three will usually just watch and listen until he becomes very familiar and comfortable with the music. Some young children may never sing songs, but simply enjoy listening.
4. Action songs are always enjoyable to young children and are especially useful whenever large muscle movement is needed in a controlled situation. Make sure the actions are literal, not symbolic.
5. Music is an ideal way to give directions or ease transitions from one part of the session to another. For example, sing "This is the way we clean up our room . . ." when it is time to move to another part of the program such as together time.
6. Children can extend many songs by thinking of appropriate additional words (see page 70).

BASIC FURNISHINGS AND EQUIPMENT FOR MUSIC ACTIVITIES

Equipment and Materials
Record player/cassette player
Autoharp
Bible with pictures
Rhythm instruments
Little Ones Sing songbook (listed on page 15)
Cassettes *Songs for 2's and 3's* and *Songs for 4's and 5's* (listed on page 15)
Other recordings, as recommended in Teacher's Manual

HOW TO SELECT APPROPRIATE SONGS

Ask the following six questions about any song you intend to use. (Some songs, like "just for fun" songs, may be useful even though not all these questions can be answered yes.)

1. **Is the meaning obvious to children?**
   Look for songs that are self-explanatory. Keep in mind that young children think literally, not symbolically. Songs such as "Climb, Climb Up Sunshine Mountain" or "This Little Light of Mine" have little meaning for children. Symbolic phrases that seem simple to adults are often confusing to children ("I was sinking deep in sin," "Come into my heart," "Let us go to the house of the Lord").

2. **Is it easily singable?**
   Children respond best to simple melody lines that are repeated. Also look for songs that are within the children's range: primarily within the six-note span from Middle C up to A.

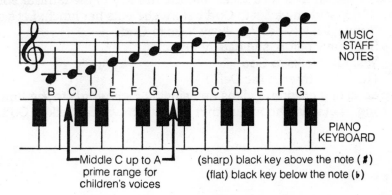

A few notes in a song may extend outside that range, but most of the melody should be within this range.

3. **Does the song relate to the current unit of Bible lessons?**
   Songs should support the aims for a unit of lessons, thus being able to be used several times in succession.

4. **Are the words scripturally and doctrinally correct?**
   Read the words carefully, and check them against the Scriptures.

5. **Does the song build positive attitudes?**
   Evaluate the mood that is created by the words, melody and rhythm. Is it consistent with your teaching goals?

6. **Will children enjoy it?**

SINGING NEW WORDS

Purpose: That children add new words to a familiar tune to express their thoughts and ideas relating to a Bible truth.

Materials
☐ Selected music—familiar song
☐ Tape recorder and cassette tape or record and record player (optional)
☐ Picture to enrich and extend a child's thinking; for example, picture of a family praying (optional)

Procedure/Conversation
1. Guide children in singing a selected familiar song such as "Jesus Loves Me," "The Farmer in the Dell," etc.
2. Use questions and comments to guide children to think and talk about the Bible aim. For example, in focusing on prayer, use questions/comments such as, "When do you talk to God, Amy? Tell me a time when your family prayed."
3. As children express their ideas, you may want to repeat the ideas for clarity and encouragement.
4. Then guide children to fit their ideas into the melody of the familiar song. For example, "Amy said she talks to God before she eats her lunch. Let's sing:
   'Amy talks to God. Yes, Amy talks to God.
   She prays before she eats her lunch.
   Yes, Amy talks to God.' "
   (Tune: "Farmer in the Dell")
5. Continue accepting children's ideas and singing their words to the tune of the familiar song. "Let's sing about another time when we can talk to God."

MUSICAL PUPPETS

Purpose: That children use puppets and music to tell about Bible-related events and ideas.

Materials
☐ Three or four puppets
☐ Selected song to extend Bible aim
☐ Tape recorder with taped song, if needed

Procedure
Example: To reinforce the Bible concept of pleasing God, use the song "Showing Love," number 84 in *Little Ones Sing* (listed on page 15).
1. Children listen and then sing as the teacher introduces the song, singing it several times.
2. Children can use the puppets to move and "sing" along.
3. Teacher guides children to think of ways they can please God by showing love. (I can help put toys away, I can make my bed each day, etc.)
4. Each puppet (child) then gets to take a turn singing the third line of the song as follows, using their own ideas:
   Teacher/children sing: How can we show our love today? How can we show our love today?
   Puppet sings: I can be kind in work and play.
   Teacher/Children sing: That's how we show our love today.
5. Sing the song several times, using the children's own words for the third line of the song.

Variations

1. Use ten finger puppets (either one set, or a set for each of three or four children who do this activity at the same time) as you sing about the ten lepers that Jesus healed. Use words like this to the tune of "Farmer in the Dell":

   > Jesus healed ten men.
   > Yes, Jesus healed ten men.
   > Only one came running back
   > Saying "thanks" for making me well.

   Children sing and move finger puppets appropriately to reinforce the events of this story.
2. You may want to use a puppet as children sing together to add interest and stimulate conversation.

Guided Conversation Ideas

Conversation you might use with the song "Showing Love": "Let's use our puppets to help us sing about ways we can show our love for others. Margie, have your puppet tell us one way we can show love. Think of something you can do for your mother at home that shows you love her. We're going to use our puppets to help us sing this song about showing love. Let's sing Margie's words when it comes to the third line." "Think about other ways we can show our love as we sing our song again."

MAKING MUSICAL INSTRUMENTS

Purpose: That children construct selected musical instruments from everyday materials and enjoy expressing their thoughts and feelings by using them.

Materials

To make a tambourine
- ☐ Paper plates
- ☐ Crayons or paints
- ☐ Stapler
- ☐ Dried beans or macaroni
- ☐ Yarn or fabric strips

To make finger cymbals
- ☐ Lids—two matching lids of each kind you use; examples: bottle caps, baby food jar lids, plastic caps from milk containers
- ☐ Flat rubber bands

Procedure

Tambourine
1. Each child uses crayons or paints to decorate two paper plates.
2. Place some dried beans or macaroni on one plate.
3. Child places the other plate face down over the first plate and staples the plates securely together along the edges, adding pieces of yarn or fabric strips for decoration.

Finger cymbals
1. Teacher punches two holes in the center of two matching lids.
2. Child folds a flat rubber band in half and pushes each end through the holes.
3. Child puts thumb and forefinger through the loops and he/she is ready to play.

Guided Conversation Ideas

"When Nehemiah and his friends finished their work, they sang and played instruments like we are making. Let's play our tambourines like Nehemiah did. We're glad we can sing and play to the Lord."

BELLS (Younger Children)

Purpose: That children listen and respond to music, using bells, and extend their awareness and enjoyment of praising God through the use of instruments.

Materials
☐ Select and use one of the following sets of bells:
- Tone bells (eight separate diatonic notes with mallets)
- Melodé bells (eight colors—hand held)

☐ Optional: cassette tape recorder or record player with tape or record

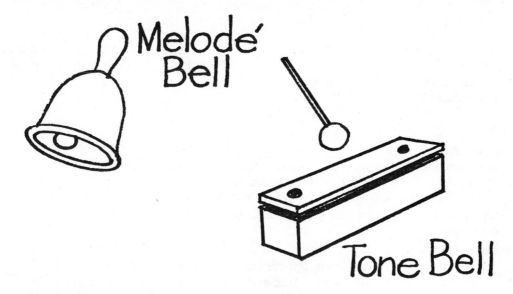

Procedure/Conversation
1. Each child takes one bell from the set.
2. "Let's see what sound each bell makes. Debbie, your bell has a high sound. How does your bell sound, Dan?"
3. "Let's listen while Debbie plays her bell. Debbie, say the words 'Thank you, Lord' and each time you say a word, play your bell."
4. "Let's all try that!"
5. "Our Bible says to thank God with music. Let's think about what we are thankful for when we play our bells."
5. "When I point to you, play your bell while we say, 'Thank you, God'." (In this way children work together to make a simple tune.)

Variations
1. Children may simply enjoy experimenting with high notes and low notes.
2. Children also enjoy listening to music and playing bells during appropriate parts of the song. (Example: "O Hear the Bells," number 100 in *Little Ones Sing*, listed on page 15)
3. Record the children's music on tape and play it back to them.

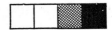

BELLS (Older Children)

Purpose: That children use bells as a means of expressing praise to God.

Materials
☐ Bells
   Use tone bells or melodé bells (see page 74). Color-code bells that are not already color-coded by placing matching colors of paper or tape on the song chart and the specific bells you are using.
☐ Song chart
   Make song chart with colored notes (gummed dots or circles cut from construction paper) to indicate which color bell is to be played.

   Example for "Oh, How I Love Jesus" (see page 76)—adjust colors to fit bells you are using.

gray	gray	blue	gray	pink	pink	
○	○	○	○	○	○	

blue	blue	pink	blue	gray	yellow	green
○	○	○	○	○	○	○

gray	gray	blue	gray	pink	pink	
○	○	○	○	○	○	

pink	blue	gray	green	gray	blue	pink
○	○	○	○	○	○	○

Procedure
1. Demonstrate how to use the bells.
2. Select children to play the bells; give one bell to each child.
3. Have child play his/her bell whenever you point to that note on chart.
4. These children give their bells to other children, who then take their turn playing the bells.

Guided Conversation Ideas
   "Let's show our love for Jesus by using these bells to play 'Oh, How I Love Jesus.' "

SONGS TO USE WITH BELLS

OH, HOW I LOVE JESUS

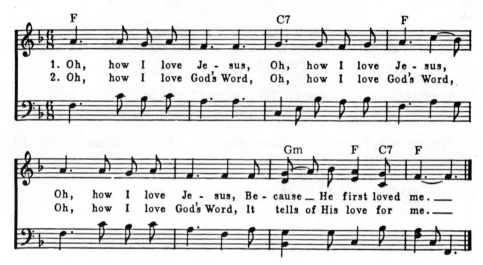

Words: Frederick Whitfield. Music: Traditional.
Arrangement © Copyright 1962 G/L Publications. Used by permission.

GOD IS SO GOOD

*Substitute one of these phrases (or similar ones): "God has made me," or "God made my hands,"
or "God made the flow'rs."

Words and Music: Traditional.

Note: Transpose this song to the key of F if you are using melode bells. You can do
this by starting the song with the bell marked "F" (instead of C) and changing the
rest of the notes accordingly (C=F, D=G, E=A, F=B♭, G=C).

MUSIC ACTIVITIES

RHYTHM INSTRUMENTS

Purpose: That children play instruments as an expression of their feelings and thoughts about God and His Word.

Materials
☐ Rhythm instruments—sticks, bells, sand blocks, triangle, cymbal, tone blocks, tambourine, drum, maracas
☐ Optional—music on record or tape

Procedure
1. Each child selects an instrument from those available.
2. He/she uses it while singing or listening to music.
3. Children should be given opportunities to try several different instruments so taking turns can be encouraged.

Variations
1. Arrange area for marching (make masking tape path on the floor).
2. Children march in single file when music begins.
3. As children pass teacher, they receive an instrument to begin using as they march. Each time they pass the teacher, they may trade instruments.
4. Near end of song teacher begins collecting instruments as children pass. Collect loudest ones first, finishing with soft sound of bell or triangle.

Guided Conversation Ideas
"Our Bible says, 'Sing songs to the Lord and play instruments,' 'Say thank you to the Lord with your hands and voices.' It pleases the Lord when we play our instruments together and sing about Him."

Children often want to use their instruments right away. You may want to have them experiment briefly so their curiosity and eagerness are satisfied.

To encourage proper use and control of the instrument, offer positive comments such as, "I like the way you use your hands to make a sound with the sand blocks." "You enjoyed using the tambourine didn't you?"

Give specific tasks for the children to do. "Play your instrument only when you hear the word 'clap'." . . . the word "help," "thanks," etc.

LISTENING/SINGING

Purpose: That children's Bible-related thoughts and feelings are extended and reinforced through listening and responding to music.

Materials
☐ Cassette tape recorder or record player
☐ Selected song on tape or record
☐ Optional—picture of children singing or picture related to Bible story or aim (hold or display at eye level)

Procedure
Children listen to the music and respond with singing, action and thoughts guided by the teacher's conversation.

Variations

Games and activities can accompany the use of music. For example, try the following game when using the song "We're Glad"—number 15 in *Little Ones Sing* (listed on page 15).

1. Prepare ahead of time, index cards with objects or ideas expressed in the five verses of this song.

2. Place cards in a pile, facedown.
3. Each child gets to pick a card (one at a time) and children sing together the corresponding verse of the song.
4. Children may want to add additional verses to the song. Have extra index cards for adding new ideas children express as they talk about things they are glad God gives us.

We're Glad

1. We're glad for the sun in the daytime,
   We're glad for the sun in the daytime,
   We're glad for the sun in the daytime,
   We're glad God made the sun.

2. stars. . .nighttime
3. good tasting carrots
4. soft cuddly kittens
5. mothers and fathers

Guided Conversation Ideas

"Listen to this song and tell me something you hear the song say that God made." "How does this song make you feel?" "Let's clap our hands as we sing the song again." "I liked the way you used your hands and voices to say thank you to God for the (sun)."

INSTRUMENTS—Autoharp

Purpose: That teacher/children use an autoharp as an accompaniment to songs that support their current unit of Bible study.

Materials
☐ Autoharp
☐ Songbooks that have autoharp chord markings above the staff—such as *Little Ones Sing,* listed on page 15. NOTE: These chord markings are sometimes transposed to a different key than the one in which the musical score is written since autoharps have a limited number of keys and chords.
☐ Autoharp cards
  ● Cut pages from an extra songbook; glue them on cardboard.
  ● Or, letter the words of the song on a large index card as in sketch. Letters above words indicate chord bar to press. Slanted marks indicate when to strum the strings. Time signature and beginning note are indicated at the left.

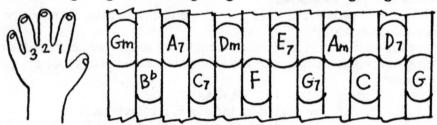

Procedure
1. Place fingers of left hand on the chord bar buttons that will be used. In "God Is So Good," finger 1 goes on C, finger 2 goes on G7, and finger 3 goes on F.

2. Press each button as indicated on song card. Cross over with your right hand and strum the strings from bottom to top.
3. Pluck string for beginning note to get your pitch for singing. For this song, you would pluck the string C. Strum autoharp as children sing.
4. Let older children take turns strumming the autoharp as rest of group sings. (You press chord buttons as they strum.)

Guided Conversation Ideas
   Example: "The Bible says, 'I will tell of the kindnesses of the Lord,. . . yes the many good things he has done' (Isa. 63:7, *NIV*). What are some kind, good things the Lord has done for you?" After children respond, say, "Let's praise God for how good He is by singing 'God Is So Good.' "

DRAMA ACTIVITIES

Drama is an enjoyable way to extend and reinforce Bible truth with young children. Included in this broad category are some of the children's favorites—block building, home living, and other roleplaying activities.

Drama-related Bible learning activities provide children with opportunities to (1) reinforce a Bible story by acting it out; (2) act out their own experiences, feelings and ideas in a natural, play-like setting. A skillful teacher will capture these moments and guide the conversation toward the learning aim. Children eagerly respond, for example, to a teacher's gentle comments about sharing lunch together around a small table set with dishes and assorted tableware.

Guidelines for Block Play

Two-year-olds enjoy blocks made of cardboard or soft foam, whereas threes, fours, and fives need wood unit blocks in a variety of shapes and lengths. (Unit blocks are so named because of the relationships in sizes of the different blocks: two smaller blocks equal the next-size block, etc.)

Plan block play in a spacious area away from traffic flow so that structures will not be toppled. A carpeted area cuts down on noise and also helps define the limits of the area.

Blocks and block equipment need to be placed where children can see them and get to them easily. Low storage shelves can be provided for this purpose.

Make sure that an adequate number of blocks is available so several children can play at one time with a minimal amount of sharing. Warm, caring adults guiding children in the block area can help children learn concepts such as sharing, kindness and helping.

Guidelines for Home Living

In this area children have the opportunity to put together and act out all the things they know about people and events they have observed and experienced. This area gives children a setting in which to (1) work together; (2) express their feelings and ideas; (3) use language to communicate their roles and respond to others' needs. For these reasons, having a home living area is especially important for giving children opportunities to understand and practice Bible truths.

Home living play also gives teachers insights into young children's thinking and feeling about themselves, other children, and the adults that care for them.

Limiting the number of children in the home living area to four or five at a time helps meaningful play to take place.

Basic equipment should first include a child-size table with several child-size chairs (see page 84). Then other kitchen-type furnishings, such as a child-size sink or stove, can be added as space and finances allow. An unlimited number of materials and items for home living play can be provided, such as doll, doll bed, kitchen dishes and utensils, dress-up clothing, etc.

BASIC FURNISHINGS AND EQUIPMENT FOR HOME LIVING

Furniture

For 2s-5s

Cabinet sink unit—24-inch (60 cm) high work surface

Stove—24 inches (60 cm) high

Table—30x40-inch (75x120 cm) surface, or round with 40-inch (100 cm) diameter

- For 2s and 3s—20 inches (50 cm) high
- For 4s and 5s—22 inches (55 cm) high

4-6 chairs

- For 2s and 3s—10 inches (25 cm) high
- For 4s and 5s—12 inches (30 cm) high

Doll bed—28x14x11 inches (70x35x27.5 cm)

Rocking chair, child-size

Ironing board, iron

Additional Furniture for 4s and 5s

Chest of drawers—24 inches (60 cm) high

Equipment and Materials

For 2s-5s

Bible with pictures

Soft plastic dishes

Doctor play materials

Dolls

- For 2s and 3s—rubber molded head
- For 4s and 5s—10-20 inches (25-50 cm) long

Two plastic telephones

Doll bedding

Dress-up clothes (male and female)

Small overnight bag

Additional Materials for 4s and 5s

Cleaning materials, child-size (mop, broom, dustpan)

Cooking utensils, child-size

Play-Doh (to use with cookie cutters, etc.)

Toy cash register and play money for playing store

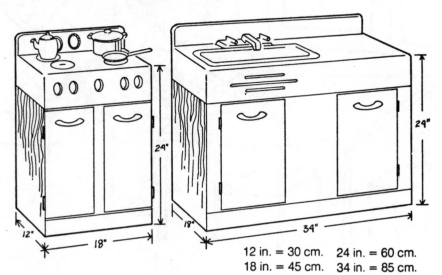

12 in. = 30 cm. 24 in. = 60 cm.
18 in. = 45 cm. 34 in. = 85 cm.

HOME LIVING—DRAMATIC PLAY

Purpose: That children relate their actions to Bible thoughts as they play and learn in a home-like setting.

Materials
☐ Child-size furnishings: table and chairs (see page 84 for sizes), doll bed or cradle, sink, stove, refrigerator, hutch, rocking chair
☐ Dolls, blankets
☐ Kitchen accessories: dishes, utensils, small pots and pans, silverware, grocery items, etc.
☐ Optional items to use from time to time: ironing board and iron (child-size), telephones, doll high chair, full length mirror, dress-up clothing, nurse or doctor kit, small suitcase, etc.

Procedure
1. Teachers provide materials that will encourage conversation related to the Bible teaching learning aim (see "Guided Conversation Ideas", page 86). Do not provide all items at all times. Change accessory materials each unit in order to focus children's thinking on that particular unit Bible teaching aim.
2. Children interact with each other in everyday experiences of home life, using the equipment and materials available.
3. Teacher guides children in their imaginative play, making appropriate comments that encourage children to talk and act in response to a Bible truth.

Guided Conversation Ideas

1. Dramatic play may be structured by the specific accessories provided. For example, a nurse or doctor kit can be used to extend the idea that God cares for us, or that He wants us to care for each other. "Have you ever been sick? How does it feel when you are sick? Who cares for you? Our Bible says to help those who are sick."

2. Dramatic play may be structured to imitate the Bible story events in a modern setting. For example, when focusing on Abraham going on a long trip, provide a suitcase with items of clothing for travel. Conversation ideas include: "Have you ever taken a long trip? Did you help to get ready for the trip? What did you pack? How did you travel? (Car, bus, plane, etc.) In Bible times Abraham took a very long trip. Do you know how he traveled? What do you think he took on his long trip? Who took care of Abraham on his long trip? Our Bible says God watched and cared for him. Who cares for you when you take a trip?"

   Another example: Blindfolds help children understand how the blind man felt when Jesus made him see. "Tell me how it feels when your eyes are covered? What happens when you try to play and you can't see? Why is it hard to be blind? How do you think the blind man felt when Jesus made him see?"

3. Children can be guided to act out Bible stories. For example: Candlesticks and some large bowls along with a dusting cloth might help children act out the story of the boy Samuel and his work in the Temple. Once again, conversation can extend a child's thoughts and actions. "Let's clean these candlesticks and bowls like Samuel did when he worked in the Temple. What are some other jobs that Samuel might have done in the Temple? What can you do to help in our church (school)?

HOME LIVING— FOOD PREPARATION

Purpose: That children extend their thoughts and ideas about God's provision of food. (The following materials and procedures are for making butter. See "Variations" on page 88 and "Recipes for Food Preparation" on pages 89, 90 for additional ideas.)

Materials
☐ Pint of heavy (whipping) cream
☐ Pint-size glass jar with lid (Why glass? It's easy for children to see what is happening.)
☐ Small dish or custard cup
☐ Small pitcher (to hold the skim milk poured off the butter)
☐ Teaspoon
☐ Table knives
☐ Salt shaker
☐ Saltines
☐ Napkins (to catch crumbs when sampling)

Procedure
Working with three or four children at one time, as we suggest for Bible learning activities, you may need to follow this procedure two or three times during the activity segment of your session. A pint of cream is ample for 12-18 children to enjoy several crackers spread with the butter that has been made. Also, you may want to try this activity at home with your family first so you have practiced the procedure and are comfortable with it.
1. Children pour about ½ to ¾ cup of cream into the glass jar and secure the lid tightly (assisted by the teacher).
2. Children take turns shaking the jar, being careful to hold it away from their chin or other children's heads.

3. As they shake the jar, children will want to watch what is happening. After a few minutes of shaking, the skim milk will separate from the butter in the jar. (Teacher may want to take a turn with a vigorous shake to speed the process.) The jar should contain a "lump" of butter surrounded by some thin milk.
4. Teacher should open the jar and pour off the skim milk into the pitcher, pressing the milk out gently with the spoon.
5. Children and teacher work together to scoop butter out into small dish. Sprinkle lightly with salt and stir.
6. Children use table knives to take a small portion of the butter and spread it on their cracker and eat. (Younger children will need the teacher to complete this part.) Delicious!

Variations

Let children prepare other foods. For example, making pudding, spreading frosting (and nuts or decorations) on cookies. See also "Recipes for Food Preparation," pages 89, 90.

Guided Conversation Ideas

Weaving conversation throughout this activity can provide many opportunities for children to think about God's provision for food and also help them see the enjoyment and value of working together. "We're going to work together today to make something delicious from cream." John, can you take this end of the carton and help me pour a little cream into this jar? As we are working, tell me something you know about cream. Yes, we do use cream to make ice cream. What else do we know about cream? One of the big reasons God made cows is to provide children and their families with milk. Cream is part of milk."

As the butter begins to form in the jar, ask, "What do you see happening inside the jar? Can you guess what we have made? When we have put the butter in the dish and added some salt, you will each get to spread some butter on a saltine and eat it. John, you can give everyone a napkin and pass the crackers as well. I'm glad God gives us butter to eat. What are some other good things God gives us to eat?"

RECIPES FOR FOOD PREPARATION

TOASTED PUMPKIN SEEDS

Ingredients

- ☐ Salt
- ☐ Vegetable oil
- ☐ Pumpkin seeds (washed and cleaned of fiber)
- ☐ Baking sheet
- ☐ Bowl

Procedure

1. Place pumpkin seeds in bowl and coat lightly with oil.
2. Spread on baking sheet and salt lightly.
3. Toast in slow oven (250-300°), stirring often to brown evenly.
4. When seeds are dry and crisp (about 30 minutes), they are ready to eat.

FRUIT TREATS

Ingredients

- ☐ Apples or bananas
- ☐ Peanut butter
- ☐ Chopped nuts (walnuts, pecans, etc.)
- ☐ Raisins
- ☐ Brown sugar (optional)

Procedure

1. Cut apples into quarters and core, or slice banana into bite-size chunks.
2. Spread pieces of fruit with peanut butter. Sprinkle raisins and nuts on top.

MOON BALLS

Ingredients

- ☐ 1 cup nonfat dry milk
- ☐ ½ cup honey
- ☐ ½ cup peanut butter
- ☐ ½ cup Granola-type cereal

Procedure

1. Mix nonfat dry milk, honey and peanut butter together.
2. Chill for an hour or more. Shape into balls and roll in Granola.

NO BAKE COOKIES

Ingredients

- ☐ ½ cup white corn syrup
- ☐ 3 cups Rice Krispies cereal
- ☐ ½ cup peanut butter

Procedure

1. Mix syrup and peanut butter together.
2. Add cereal and mix until cereal is evenly coated.
3. Spoon onto wax paper or pat into an 8x8-inch buttered pan and cut into squares.

(continued on next page)

SCRAMBLED EGGS (enough for a class of 15 children)

Ingredients

- [ ] 1 dozen eggs
- [ ] ½ cup milk
- [ ] Salt
- [ ] 3 tbsps. butter or margarine
- [ ] Electric frying pan
- [ ] Cooking spatula and egg beater
- [ ] Medium-size bowl
- [ ] Small paper plates and spoons

Procedure

1. Preheat frying pan (low to medium setting).
2. Break eggs into bowl. Add milk. Beat with egg beater until foamy.
3. Place butter in the preheated frying pan and cook eggs until firm.
4. Salt lightly and serve.
5. It is best to work with 3 to 5 children at a time, cooking just 3 or 4 eggs with each group. Involve the children as much as possible in preparing the eggs!

APPLESAUCE

Ingredients

- [ ] 6 or 8 apples
- [ ] ½ cup water
- [ ] Large saucepan and bowl
- [ ] Food strainer
- [ ] 2 tbsps. sugar or honey
- [ ] 1 tbsp. cinnamon (optional)
- [ ] Large spoon and cutting knife

Procedure

1. Wash the apples. Cut them into small pieces and remove the cores.
2. Place the cut up fruit into saucepan with ½ cup water.
3. Cook and stir over low heat for about 15 minutes until the apples become mushy.
4. Remove from heat and put cooked apples through the food strainer.
5. Add sugar and cinnamon and applesauce is ready to eat!

BUTTER COOKIES

Ingredients

- [ ] 1 cup butter or margarine
- [ ] 2 cups flour
- [ ] ¼ cup sugar or honey
- [ ] 2 tbsps. vanilla
- [ ] Bowl and large spoon
- [ ] Measuring cups and spoons
- [ ] Cookie sheets
- [ ] Chopped nuts (optional)

Procedure

1. Cream the butter and sugar together. Add flour and vanilla.
2. Shape into ½-inch balls and flatten slightly on cookie sheet.
3. Bake at 350° for 10 to 15 minutes.

HEALTHFUL SNACK IDEAS THAT CHILDREN CAN HELP PREPARE

- [ ] Shelled sunflower seeds
- [ ] Fresh fruit slices
- [ ] Vegetable slices with dip
- [ ] Cheese and crackers
- [ ] Granola (try making your own)
- [ ] Banana dipped in sesame seeds

HOME LIVING—HELPING

Purpose: That children roleplay a way they can help at home by matching table setting items to a place mat design.

Materials
- ☐ Construction paper (for place mat)—12x18 inches (30x45 cm)
- ☐ Marking pen (dark color)
- ☐ Paper or plastic plate (luncheon size)
- ☐ Paper or plastic cup
- ☐ Table knife, fork, and teaspoon
- ☐ Paper napkin (folded)

Procedure
1. Before class, use marking pen to trace around table-setting items to make outline shapes on the place mat (see sketch).
2. Put the table-setting items and place mat on a table for children to use.
3. Children match the table-setting items to the appropriate shape outlined on the place mat.

Variations
Other helping activities children can roleplay include washing/drying dishes, sweeping the floor, taking care of a baby, ironing, dusting, taking out the trash, etc.

Guided Conversation Ideas
Help me put this fork where it belongs on the place mat. Touch the place for the napkin. Touch where we put the plate. What goes in this place? (Touch the cup outline.) You can help set the table here and you can help at home, too. I'm glad you are a helper today. It pleases me to see you helping. God is pleased when you are a helper, too. Tell me how you help your family get ready to eat."

BASIC FURNISHING AND EQUIPMENT FOR BLOCK BUILDING

Furniture
For 2s-5s
Open shelves with closed back—12
    inches (30 cm) deep

Additional Furniture for 2s and 3s
Balance beam—4-6 inches (10-15 cm)
    wide

Equipment and Materials
For 2s-5s
Bible with pictures
Blocks (large cardboard for 2s, wooden
    unit blocks for 3s through 5s)
Sturdy wooden trucks, cars, etc.
Block accessories (people, animals, etc.)

Additional Materials for 2s and 3s
Balls—7-9 inches (17.5-22.5 cm)
    in diameter

BLOCK BUILDING

Purpose: That children demonstrate and express Bible story concepts or Bible-related actions while constructing with blocks.

Materials
☐ Hardwood unit blocks (cardboard blocks with two-year-olds)
☐ Cars, trucks, and other play vehicles
☐ Family, animal figures (wood, plastic or other unbreakable material)

Procedure/Conversation
Children select blocks and use them to build structures and other imaginative patterns representing their experiences and ideas (roleplaying).

1. An everyday theme is easily roleplayed by the children using blocks. For example, in extending the theme of coming to church/school, the following conversation would be appropriate: "I'm glad you came to church/school today. Tell me how you got here. Did you walk? Let's make a car here with the blocks. Phil, you be the dad driving to church. Your dad cares about you to drive you and your family to church. It's good to go to church and learn about God.

2. A Bible story theme can be extended in the block area as well. For example, "Our Bible tells us of a boy named Joseph who obeyed his father. Let's pretend I am your dad. I'm going to tell you to do something, and you can obey. Todd, put this truck over there on the blue carpet. Thank you for obeying. Our Bible says, 'Children obey your parents.' I'm glad Joseph obeyed his father, and I'm glad we can obey, too."

3. Using supplementary pieces provided in the block area can be helpful in extending the dramatic play. The wooden people support children's play in relating everyday experiences to Bible truth. For example, "This little girl has fallen and hurt her leg. How can we help her? Let's build something together that will help care for her. Our Bible says we should care about others."

4. Events from the Bible story can be acted out, or objects from the Bible story can be constructed: Solomon's Temple, a well, a fishing boat, etc.

SAND/RICE TABLE

Purpose: That children enjoy working together with sand or rice contained in a large box-like table.

Materials
☐ Sand or rice (enough to cover 2 inches of the bottom of the table). You may prefer rice, as it is easier to manage and also easier to clean up if spilled.
☐ Sand (rice) table—purchased from a school supply company or handmade
☐ Plastic containers, funnels, plastic spoons, etc. (try using just shells of all shapes and sizes)

Procedure
Children use the materials provided to work in the sand or rice. They talk and share actions and ideas with two or three other children involved in this activity at the same time.

Variations

1. As a child approaches five or six years old, it is increasingly possible to use a Bible story or theme in relation to the sand (rice) table activity. For example, children can walk the people of Israel (chenille wire people that children have made) across the wilderness.
2. The sand (rice) table lends itself to increasing children's understanding of life and customs in Bible times (a nomadic scene, a village scene, etc.).
3. Fill a child's wading pool with shredded paper. Children enjoy sitting, hiding and crawling in the paper.

Guided Conversation Ideas

Anyone who has seen children at the beach knows how engrossed they become in playing with sand. The versatility of sand (rice) provides a framework for the development of many kinds of concepts, including spiritual ones. A sand table provides unlimited opportunities for children to cooperate, share and develop a sensitivity toward working side by side with others. It is the teacher's conversation that can guide this play toward biblical attitudes and responses.

"I see Billy needs a spoon to move his rice. Charles, what can you do to help? Thank you, Charles, for sharing your tools."

"We're going to take turns with the orange dish. I'll go first, and then in a few minutes I'll share it with someone else. I'm glad we can work together in the rice table."

FLANNELBOARD

Purpose: That children arrange flannel figures or felt shapes on a flannelboard to reinforce a Bible story or Bible concept, helping them recall Bible information and better understanding God's truth.

Materials
☐ Flannelboard—tabletop size about 12x18 inches (30x45 cm). (A flannelboard can easily be made by covering cardboard with flannel material, gluing it in place in the back.)
☐ Flannel-backed figures, either commercially made or prepared by the teacher.

Procedure
1. Teacher selects flannel-backed figures which convey or portray a certain Bible story or Bible concept.
2. The number of figures available to work with at one time should be limited. Two- and three-year-olds may need just four or five pieces at once, whereas fours and fives might handle six or eight flannel figures effectively. Select the pieces that will enable children to recall or understand the most important aspects of the Bible story.
3. Children arrange and manipulate the flannel-backed figures on the flannelboard.

Guided Conversation Ideas
Teacher conversation is very effective in this activity. Children will be eager to "tell" parts of the story (or share their ideas about a Bible theme) with just a little encouragement from the teacher and some well-worded open questions. Examples from the Bible story about Jesus making a little girl well again (Matthew 9) are: "Tell me what the sad father said to Jesus." "What happened when Jesus went into the little girl's house?" "What did Jesus do?" "Move your figure to show me what happened next." "What did people think about Jesus?" "If you had been there that day, what would you have said about Jesus?" "How did Jesus show He cared about the little girl?"

PLAY THE STORY

Purpose: That children:
● show/reinforce their understanding of what happened in a Bible event;
● portray the feelings of Bible characters in preparation for discussing (1) their own feelings in a similar situation; (2) ways to live out a Bible truth in this type of situation.

Materials

Children can act out stories without any costumes, props or scenery, but these items often stimulate their interest and add to their enjoyment (see "Variations" on page 98). Use as time permits.

Procedure

1. Tell the story, using conversation as well as description.
2. Review the story with the group. Guide them to think through the story and sequence of events by asking questions:
    a. What happened first in the story?
    b. Who were the people? What did they say?
    c. How do you think they felt? How can you show this?
    d. What happened next in the story?
3. Decide who will play each character. If several children wish to play the same part, play story several times, taking turns.
4. Act out the story. If a child pauses, ask a question to help him/her remember the action of the story.

Variations

1. Let children use costumes and props in acting out the story.
2. Let older children make scenery to use in the story. Supply shelf paper, poster board, crayons, paint, brushes, scissors, glue, tape.

Guided Conversation Ideas

After playing the story, ask questions to help children relate the Bible truth to everyday living. For example, after children act out the story of Abraham giving Lot first choice, ask such questions as, "What are some times when it is hard for you to give someone else first choice?"

BASIC EQUIPMENT FOR PUPPETS

Student-Made Puppets

See pages 37 and 41 for finger puppets and paper bag puppets your children will enjoy making.

Puppet Box

Enlist the help of parents and other adults in making additional puppets for children to use in puppet Bible learning activities. Step-by-step instructions and patterns for puppets can be found in *Easy-to-Make Puppets and How to Use Them: Early Childhood,* by Fran Rottman, Regal Books, Ventura, CA. Examples of some of these puppets are shown below.

Store puppets in a box that has been covered with colorful paper.

DRAMA ACTIVITIES

PUPPETS—Bible Times

Purpose: That children use puppets to:
- show/reinforce their understanding of what happened in a Bible event;
- portray the feelings of Bible characters in preparation for discussing (1) their own feelings in a similar situation; (2) ways to live out a Bible truth in this type of situation.

Materials
☐ Bible times puppets (children can make their own or use puppets from Puppet Box)—see pages 37, 41, 99.

Procedure
Follow the steps outlined for "Play the Story," page 97. Children who have difficulty expressing their feelings will be better able to put feelings into words and actions when using a simple puppet.

Guided Conversation Ideas
After playing the story, ask questions to help children relate the Bible truth to everyday living. For example, after children act out the story of Joseph's jealous brothers, ask questions such as, "What made Joseph's brothers feel jealous? Everyone feels jealous at some time or other. Sometimes people feel jealous when they want something someone else has. Sometimes they feel jealous because they want to be able to do something someone else can do. Think about a time when you have felt jealous of someone—when you have wanted something someone else had—or when you wanted to be able to do something someone else could do. The Bible tells us, "When others are happy, be happy with them" (Romans 12:15, *TLB*). Why is this sometimes hard to do? What can you do when you find it hard to be happy with someone who has received something you wish you had?"

PUPPETS—Present-Day

Purpose: That children use puppets to:

● express feelings and actions of present-day people as they (the children) think through problem situations;

● demonstrate ways of obeying God's commands and acting on God's promises.

Materials

☐ Present-day puppets (children can make their own or use puppets from Puppet Box)—see pages 37, 41, 99.

Procedure

1. Read a Bible verse
2. Guide children to (a) tell about situations when they need to remember this Bible verse; (b) select one situation to act out. Or, suggest an open-ended situation (a problem situation that needs to be solved in light of this verse).
3. Guide children to think through the situation by asking questions:
   a. What happens first?
   b. Who are the people? What do they say?
   c. How do they feel? How can you show this?
   d. What happens next?
4. Decide who will play each character.
5. Children either make simple puppets or choose puppets from Puppet Box.
6. Children use puppets to act out the story. If a child pauses, ask a question to help him/her remember the action of the story.
7. Guide children to evaluate the results by asking questions such as, "How did (name of puppet) obey/not obey the Bible command we read? What's another way he/she might have obeyed this command? What are some ways you can obey this command at home? at school? at church?"

Variations

See "Musical Puppets," page 71.

Guided Conversation Ideas

Example of an open-ended situation for use in teaching John 15:12—"Your little sister got into your new box of crayons and broke them. How do you feel about this? What will you do about it?"

COMMUNICATION ACTIVITIES

All Bible learning activities involve conversation to insure their effectiveness with young children, but there are some activities in which the central idea focuses on verbal communication. Included in this category are such activities as nature walks (see page 65) and field trips, where children talk and plan for the event and then discuss what happened following the trip. All of these Bible learning activities use some type of communication to focus a child's thoughts on Bible truth.

Some of the Bible learning activities in this category involve the use of simple audiovisual equipment that is especially effective with the older preschool child. Four- and five-year-olds can operate a simple cassette player (play, stop, rewind) while listening to a Bible story that has been recorded.

Individual headsets add to the enjoyment and privacy of the learning experience. These listening centers can also become viewing centers with the addition of short, appropriate filmstrips for children. A teacher's guidance is needed not only to operate the filmstrip machine, but also to guide the conversation with comments and questions that encourage children to talk about what they are seeing and hearing.

Cassette tapes, filmstrips and books for this type of activity can be purchased from church suppliers and local Christian bookstores.

It is also fun to record your own clear reading of a Bible story on a cassette tape (use a sound such as a bell as a signal for turning each page in the book).

Make sure that all materials you use with audiovisual equipment is suitable to the interest and ability level of the children you teach.

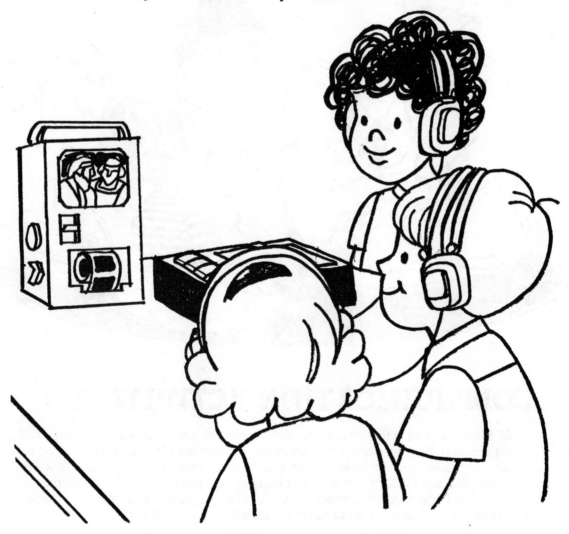

Here are some guidelines to follow in making communication Bible learning activities effective with young children.

1. Avoid using symbolic or adult-oriented terms and ideas with preschool children. For example, young children seldom understand phrases like "God provides for our needs," "bowing down to idols," "the Bible is the Word of God," or "Jesus saves."

2. Children enjoy having their own words and thoughts represented in print by an adult. Letter children's words on large paper as they express their ideas to you or to other children. Read back to them what they have said as you point to each word.

3. Use visuals to increase interest and further understanding. Remember, "a picture is worth a thousand words." Hold or display visuals at eye level. Involve children in focusing on the message conveyed by the visual. Use questions such as:

   "What does this picture tell us?"
   "What do you think the man will do next?"
   "How is this boy pleasing God?"
   "How did Jesus show love in this picture?"

4. For young children, telling the Bible story during a Bible learning activity is often helpful. Teachers can use this informal opportunity to relate the Bible story, or parts of the Bible story, to small groups of children. As children casually gather on the floor around the teacher, the story may be repeated several times with eager listeners. Some guidelines for storytelling are:

   ● Focus on the main character and how he/she reaches his/her goal.

   ● Use questions, particularly at the beginning, to focus a child's attention and capture his interest.

   ● Excitement and enthusiasm in your voice is important. Loudness and softness can be used effectively to make a point.

   ● Use descriptive adjectives and lots of action words to help children paint a mental picture.

   ● Make use of a dialogue. Say the words as you think the character might have said them.

   ● Ability to retain Bible information increases with age. Repetition is not only enjoyed by children, but is also necessary for long-term retention of Bible information. This will in no way interfere with children's interest during story time, since children like best the stories they know best!

BOOKS

Purpose: That children enjoy looking at books selected to reinforce and support the learning aim.

Materials

☐ Variety of children's books selected to reinforce and support the learning aim. It is best to choose books with simple, colorful pictures and very few words on a page. Children benefit most from books that match their interest and experiences. Two-year-olds may still need books with stiff, heavy pages for durability.

☐ Child-size book display rack (see sketch below), low shelves or table.

☐ Optional materials:
   Rocking chair
   Comfortable bean bag chair
   Carpet remnant pieces
   Pictures of children looking at books; post pictures at children's eye level.

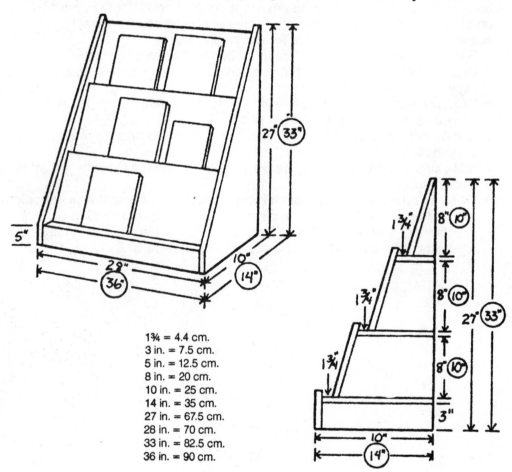

1¾ = 4.4 cm.
3 in. = 7.5 cm.
5 in. = 12.5 cm.
8 in. = 20 cm.
10 in. = 25 cm.
14 in. = 35 cm.
27 in. = 67.5 cm.
28 in. = 70 cm.
33 in. = 82.5 cm.
36 in. = 90 cm.

Procedure

1. Place in a quiet area books related to the unit Bible aim. For example, with a unit on Creation provide books about animals/trees/plants and Bible story books on God's creation. A unit on "Jesus Helps People" might include books about Jesus' ministry as well as books about children and their everyday experiences of sharing and helping. It is better to have three or four carefully-selected books available than to have a wide variety of books out at one time.
2. Children freely choose from the books offered.
3. Children page through the book they select and enjoy the illustrations and colorful pictures.
4. With guided conversation from the teacher, children are stimulated to think and talk about the Bible aim.

Guided Conversation Ideas

"What do you see on this page, Brenda? Touch the girl who is helping. Tell me what you think this mother might be saying. Let's turn the page and see what happens. Who else is a helper here? What is he doing? What do you do at home to help?"

A teacher in the book area is naturally drawn to reading the book to the children, which children always enjoy. Be sure to include some conversation and open questions to encourage a child's thoughts and responses.

Try telling the story in your own words as the child turns the pages. Or, better still, encourage the child to talk about each page as you "read" together.

FIELD TRIP

Purpose: That children increase their understanding of Bible truths and extend Bible content into life-related experiences.

Materials

☐ Materials needed for the specific field trip to be taken (for example, Valentines to be taken to nursing home, containers for specimens children find on a nature walk, etc.)

Advance Preparation

☐ Contact person or place to be visited.

☐ Inform parents of your plans at least two weeks in advance (parents need to know that their child will be leaving his or her classroom).

☐ Arrange for transportation (if necessary).

Procedure/Conversation

Field trips need to be planned with children well in advance. Anticipation and conversation preceding the event can greatly increase the effectiveness and enjoyment of the trip. Plan your trip based on an aim you wish to extend with your class. Examples of field trips that may extend Bible truths:

1. A trip to a nearby nursing home to deliver valentines helps children understand and experience showing love to others. Talking ahead of time with the children is important. "When we made these valentines, we talked about sharing them with other people to show that we care for these people. God loves and cares for everyone and He wants us to show our love, too. Sometimes people who are very old live in special buildings called nursing homes. I think these people would enjoy getting a valentine from us. Tell me about someone you know who is old and can't go outside. How do you think a very old person might feel if we brought a valentine to him/her?"

2. Walking to a nearby park, meadow, or garden can increase children's awareness of God's creation. Conversation, again, is the key to success. "When we take our walk we will see, hear and smell many things. Let's think of some things we might see that God made. I'll write the words here as you say them to me." (Write children's ideas on a large sheet of paper. This can also be done following the trip.) While walking through the park, teachers' casual conversation is important. "What do you notice about the grass? I hear something chirping that's up high. I see something yellow that God made. Why does God give us trees? Thank you, God, for trees."

3. Visiting in the home of a child with a long-term illness or injury helps children develop a sensitivity and love for other children. Children will want to take along some class papers and handmade cards they have signed. "What are some things we can say to our friend Carol when we visit her next week? How do you think Carol will feel when we come to her door? What do you think she will say? Visiting Carol is one way we can show our love. God tells us to love each other. Let's pray now that God will help Carol to feel better."

Variation

Plan a field trip or other event at a time other than class time. For example, children benefit from a brief visit to the church auditorium to hear hymns played on the organ.

PICTURE GUESSING GAME

Purpose: That children play a picture guessing game to focus on the details of a particular Bible story visual.

Materials
☐ Picture of a familiar Bible story
☐ Glue
☐ Construction paper
☐ Manila envelope—the size of the picture when mounted

Procedure
1. Before class, glue the picture on the construction paper and place it in the manila envelope.
2. Children watch as you pull a few inches of the picture out of the envelope. Then they guess what the picture might be.
3. Continue to gradually reveal more of the picture until the children have guessed something about the Bible story illustrated in the picture.
4. Several pictures may be prepared in this way, allowing the children to enjoy playing the game with different Bible stories.

Variation
1. Children also enjoy playing this guessing game to identify pictures of things God made.
2. Five-year-olds may want to draw their own pictures to use in this game.

Guided Conversation Ideas
"I have a picture in this envelope. We're going to play a game to see if we can discover something about the picture. Let's pull the picture out of the envelope just a tiny bit. What do you see? Can you tell me something about this picture from this little part that you see? Good, Amy, you noticed something blue. What could it be? Let's pull the picture out of the envelope a little more. What do you see now? How can you tell that this is part of a boat? Tell me who you think will be in this picture from what you see so far. Let's pull out more of the picture and you tell me what you see."

TELEPHONE TALK

Purpose: That children use telephones to talk about a Bible story and extend their knowledge of Bible content.

Materials
☐ Two telephones (not hooked up)

Procedure/Conversation
Guided by teacher questions and encouraging statements, children "talk" to each other, using the telephones provided. (It is suggested that the telephones be in two separate areas of the room, but close enough that children can hear each other).

For example, children enjoy recalling and relating the adventurous details of the story of Noah. "Tammy is listening on the other phone. She'd like to hear about Noah. Tell her what our Bible says about Noah."

Variation
Teacher may want to talk on the telephone to encourage children to recall Bible truths. "How did God keep Noah safe from the water? What happened when Noah and his family left the ark?"

BIBLE THOUGHT TOSS

Purpose: That children repeat a Bible thought while tossing a bean bag.

Materials
☐ Bean bag
☐ Carpeted floor area away from traffic

Procedure
1. Two or three children and the teacher sit on the floor in a small circle.
2. The teacher tosses bean bag to one child while saying the first word of a Bible thought such as "Jesus Loves Me."
3. Teacher guides the child who received the bean bag to say the second word of the Bible thought "loves," while tossing the bean bag to another child.
4. That child is then helped to complete the Bible thought by saying the word "me," while tossing the bean bag to the remaining child or back to the teacher.
5. Repeat the activity often as it becomes familiar and enjoyable. Examples of other Bible thoughts to use with this activity:
   "God is so good"
   "Jesus is my friend"
   "Happy Birthday, Jesus"

Guided Conversation Ideas
"We're going to toss this bean bag as we say the Bible thought 'Jesus loves me.' I'm going to say the first word, 'Jesus,' as I toss the bean bag to Jeff. Now, Jeff, when you toss the bean bag to a friend, say the next word in our Bible thought, 'loves.' Good toss, Jeff! Carla, what's the last word of our Bible thought? Who does Jesus love, Carla? Good, you remembered. Let's try it again."

STORYTELLING

Purpose: That the learners will have an opportunity to participate in telling the Bible story.

Materials
☐ Bibles
☐ Pictures (optional)

Procedure
1. Assist children in the selection of the Bible story that they will prepare to tell.
2. The story may be told to another small group within the class or to a group of younger children.
3. Children may wish to combine this activity with an art activity by making simple illustrations or puppets to help to tell the story.
4. Provide time to practice the story.
5. Arrange for the storytelling time and place.

Variations
1. Provide a tape recorder and blank cassette. Learners may record their Bible stories. The stories can be shared with absent children or kept in the room for a resource for a Bible learning activity.
2. The tape and tape recorder can be used in a listening center.

Guided Conversation Ideas
Encourage learners to be aware of sequence by asking, "What happened next?" Help the storytellers include some dialogue in their stories by asking, "What did _____ say when _____ ?" "What does this story help us understand about something God wants us to do?" will encourage the learners to think about the application of Bible truth in their daily lives.

DICTATE (Adult Record)

Purpose: That the child express information, ideas and/or feelings for an adult to put into written form.

Materials
- ☐ Paper
- ☐ Pencils
- ☐ Typewriter (optional)
- ☐ Cassette recorder and blank tape (optional)

Procedure
1. Child talks about a picture, an item or a Bible event.
2. An adult worker records what the child says.

Variations
1. The child may dictate his ideas to a tape recorder. The adult writes the child's dictation from the tape.
2. The adult may type what the child is saying as it is being said. Many adults can type as fast as children talk, even though they may not be accomplished typists. The child will enjoy watching his words become print. Perhaps the child can type his/her own name.

Guided Conversation Ideas
If the child is telling about a picture or event, suggest that he/she answer the question, "What is the most important thing to know about it?" "How would you describe it?" Avoid questions that can be answered Yes or No. They do not stimulate thinking.

PICTURE STUDY

Purpose: That the child gain information or answer questions as he looks at pictures.

Materials
☐ Bibles
☐ Pictures (may be in books)

Procedure
1. Picture study needs to involve looking and talking.
2. Ask the child to look at the picture(s) and (a) talk about what is happening or (b) describe the clothes Bible people are wearing or (c) name the people and tell what they are doing.
3. The content of the conversation will be determined by the picture and the specific information to be learned from it.

Variations
1. Categorize and file pictures according to content or purpose. From a collection of pictures, ask the child to find all the pictures that show a way Jesus helped someone. Place them in a designated place.
2. Look at pictures that show situations that involve children today. Ask child to tell or show what might happen next.
3. Place pictures in sequence. For example, use several pictures that show some part of the birth of Jesus. One way to show sequence is to clip pictures to a clothesline.

Guided Conversation Ideas
"Look at these three pictures. Choose the one that shows the best thing to do when you are angry." "Look at these three pictures. Lay them on the table in a way to show what happened first and second, etc. When they are in order, clip them to the clothesline."

FILMS/FILMSTRIPS

Purpose: That children add to ideas and information or explore feelings as they watch and listen to a film/filmstrip presentation.

Materials
- ☐ Projector
- ☐ Film/filmstrip
- ☐ Cassette player/tape

Procedure
1. Preview film/filmstrip before class.
2. Thread projector/cassette player. Check to see that focus and volume are set for correct viewing and listening.
3. Talk with children about what they may expect to learn. Ask questions and give specific suggestions for ideas and events to expect.
4. Follow the film/filmstrip with questions and discussion.

Variations
1. Show a portion of the film/filmstrip without sound and ask the children to provide the narration or conversation.
2. Stop the film/filmstrip at a point of decision and ask learners what they think might happen next.

Guided Conversation Ideas
   Conversation needs to be centered around the information, concepts and ideas presented or reinforced in the film/filmstrip. Question in a way that will lead children to explore their feelings about concepts.

GAMES AND PUZZLES

Games and puzzles for young children involve materials that can be moved, explored, manipulated or combined, helping children to focus their energy and attention toward certain goals. Some activities simply foster enjoyment of the task and positive attitudes toward church/school—for example, beads and laces and nesting boxes. Two- and three-year-olds especially are in need of this type of activity. Other activities may have specific Bible-related goals in addition to fostering enjoyment of task and positive attitudes.

Whatever the game or puzzle activity provided, children's strong need for involvement and direct experiences is being met. Mentally, a child is challenged to think, recall, and sort information, responding with appropriate or creative use of materials. Socially and emotionally, children derive great satisfaction from interacting with one another in their tasks.

Here are some guidelines for using this type of Bible learning activity with young children.

1. Manipulative materials (Lego, puzzles, etc.) should be made available selectively. If the same table materials are offered week after week with no variety, change or relationship to aim, children will lose interest in them. Children may even misuse them (throwing, dumping pieces, etc.). Make sure that these materials are varied and that they are accompanied by a teacher's aim-related conversation so they do not lose their effectiveness and value in the classroom.

2. Keep in mind that some game and puzzle learning activities have some characteristics of other types of activities such as art or drama. For example, some putting-together/taking-apart material might be part of block building. And sometimes, when children make their own puzzles, this becomes partly an art activity.

3. Wooden puzzles vary in their degree of difficulty. We suggest investing in puzzles that have places and things that are realistic to children of that age. Select puzzles with the following number of pieces:

> two-year-olds (whole objects): 2-6
> three-year-olds: 6-10
> four- and five-year-olds: 8 or more

A puzzle rack is an excellent investment for puzzle storage. Children can then use one puzzle at a time and be responsible for returning it to its proper place when they have finished.

NOTE: Bible-related hardwood puzzles are available from The Judy Company. These are recommended as excellent resources to reinforce and extend Bible truths with young children. Send for a catalog (see address on page 14).

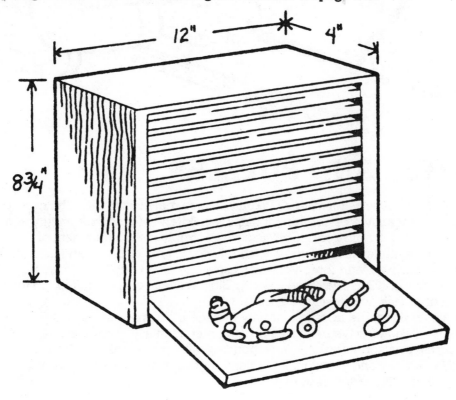

4. Felt boards can easily be made for child use. Cover a 10 x 12-inch (25 x 30 cm) piece of plywood or very heavy poster board with a solid piece of felt or flannel. You can make your own felt pieces or purchase them from school and church suppliers.

5. Encourage children to talk about what they are doing during game and puzzle activities. For example, "I noticed you made two designs. How is this one different from that one?" Help children discover ways they can carry out Bible-related ideas of helping and sharing. Conversation such as this helps: "Matt looks as if he needs something. What can you do to help?" "There are some pegs on the floor, Julie. I'll get the red ones by my foot; you can pick up the rest."

6. Many Bible-related games can be teacher-made. These help children to think and talk about Bible truths. By the time a child turns five, he is able to understand the procedures of most simple games and can easily participate except for reading print.

PUZZLES

Purpose: That children use puzzles to focus their attention toward a Bible learning aim.

Materials

☐ Selected hardwood puzzles relating to a Bible aim. For example, when learning about David the shepherd, a puzzle with a sheep would be appropriate. When learning about God's gift of food, provide puzzles with fruits, vegetables and other food-related objects and scenes.

Procedure

1. Selected puzzles are placed either on a table or on low shelves where children can have free access to them.
2. Children choose a puzzle from among those offered. After removing the pieces from the base, children begin to arrange the pieces in their places, using shape, position and color clues to complete the puzzle successfully.
3. To help a child enjoy and be successful at puzzles.
   - avoid finishing a puzzle for him/her. (You may want to take turns fitting in pieces.)
   - place the pieces to the left of the base to encourage good eye-hand coordination.
   - turn a piece right side up or move it near its position to help a child see where it might fit.

SEQUENCING PICTURES

Purpose: That children place a series of pictures in order, depicting events of a selected Bible story so as to extend and reinforce their understanding of that Bible story.

Materials

☐ Series of pictures (showing different events in a Bible story) mounted on large index cards. You may want to cover the cards with clear plastic.

- Use three or four pictures with three-year-olds and young fours.
- Use up to eight pictures with five-year-olds.
- Example: Pictures for the story of Noah might include these events:
  Noah building the ark
  People making fun of Noah's work
  Animals entering the ark
  Ark floating; rain coming down
  Noah sending out the dove
  Ark resting on the mountain
  Noah thanking God; rainbow
- Sources for pictures: "Adventure Through the Bible" series for grades 3-6, available from GL Publications, Ventura, CA; old Bible storybooks with at least four clear illustrations of one complete story; hand-illustrated scenes using simple figures.

Procedure/Conversation

Guide children as they place each picture in the order in which the events occurred in the Bible story. "Look at these cards with pictures of our Bible story about Noah. Tell me which one you think shows what happened first. Tell me what Noah is doing in this picture. (Building a boat.) Why is he doing that? (He's obeying God, or God told him to.) What did people think about this special job God gave Noah? Look at the picture and tell me what these people might be saying. Choose what picture you think comes next. Tell me what you see in this picture."

Continue asking open questions and making directed comments throughout this activity, guiding children's thinking toward the Bible aim. "How did God take care of Noah? What did Noah do to show that he loved God? What did the rainbow mean?"

MANIPULATIVE MATERIALS

Purpose: That children enjoy using materials to explore, build, sort, put together and take apart.

Materials
Examples to choose from:
- ☐ Beads and laces
- ☐ Wooden picture dominoes
- ☐ Nesting cups and boxes
- ☐ Pegs and pegboards
- ☐ Tinkertoys
- ☐ Interlocking plastic squares, cylinders, etc.
- ☐ Lego, Duplo, interlocking blocks, etc.
- ☐ Shape sorters
- ☐ Wooden puzzles
- ☐ Bristle blocks
- ☐ Nuts and Bolts (plastic)

NOTE: Since original cartons are seldom appropriate for use by children, here are some suggestions for storing manipulative materials:
- ☐ Wicker bread baskets
- ☐ Shoe boxes or large coffee cans covered with contact paper
- ☐ Clear plastic shoe boxes with lids
- ☐ Plastic dishpan or "tote" trays available from school suppliers

Procedure

1. Children select manipulative materials from those which have been placed on a table or stored on low shelves.
2. Children put together, take apart, build or explore (depending on the material available), guided by the teacher. For example, manipulatives such as Lego and pegboards with pegs involve children in putting together and taking apart, whereas with wooden puzzles and picture dominoes a definite pattern can be explored.

Guided Conversation Ideas

Encourage appropriate use of materials: "I like what you have done with those pegs. It looks as if you are enjoying your work. You know how to line up the red ones on this side. There are some pegs on the floor next to your chair. I think you can reach them and put them in the basket."

Encourage and extend a child's understanding of helping and sharing: "I'm glad you left some blue pegs for Brian. Thank you for sharing. Megan needs just one more green peg to finish her design. How can you help her? Why don't you and Julie work together on this puzzle? First, you find a piece that fits and then Julie can find a piece. You can take turns and help each other."

PAPER PLATE HAPPY FACE

Purpose: That children make a happy-face puzzle, using a paper plate.

Materials
- ☐ Paper plates
- ☐ Crayons or marking pens
- ☐ Blunt scissors
- ☐ Optional: paper bags to hold cut-up puzzle pieces

Procedure
1. Children use crayons or marking pens to make features of a face, or teacher prepares smiling face on paper plates ahead of time.
2. Guided by the teacher, children use the scissors to cut paper plate apart into three or four pieces of about the same size.
3. Children then take the pieces and fit them together again to make a happy face.

Guided Conversation Ideas
"I like your happy smile today, Barbara. I'm glad you came to school/church today because we're going to have some fun with smiling faces. Use this crayon to make a face that has a big smile. When you're finished, you'll get to make a puzzle of your happy face. I'll hold the paper plate still while you use these scissors to cut. How many pieces do you have now? Let's put them together to make a happy face. Good work, Barbara! You fit that piece right by the eye where it belongs."

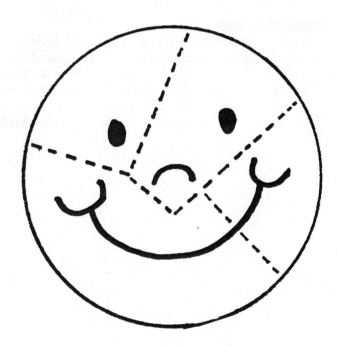

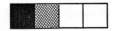

MATCHING GAME

Purpose: That children recall Bible stories by matching two pieces of a simple picture together.

Materials
☐ Four or five simple Bible story pictures
- cut from used Sunday School papers
- covered with clear plastic
- each cut in two pieces (varying the shape)

☐ Shallow box or envelope (marked "Matching Game") into which you put the picture pieces (mixed up)

Procedure
1. Children put the 8-10 picture pieces out in front of them.
2. They match the pieces together to form complete pictures.
3. Teacher asks questions about the pictures to guide the child's thinking toward the Bible teaching/learning aim.

Variations
1. Use pictures of everyday experiences to extend a child's understanding of Bible concepts such as sharing, helping, and obeying.
2. Draw pictures of Bible objects which can be matched. Examples: for the story of David the shepherd—harp, sheep, David, lion; for the story of feeding the crowds—fish, loaves of bread, baskets, crowds, Jesus, little boy.

Guided Conversation Ideas
"Look at these picture pieces and see if you can tell which ones belong together. Find something green that might match this tree. Yes, you found two pieces that make a whole picture. What do you see in this picture? What do you think the little girl is saying? What do you think the man that Jesus helped will do next? Let's see if we can find some other pieces that match. This picture reminds me of when God made the world. Touch something that God made that is yellow. What else do you see that God made?"

"PLEASING GOD" LOTTO

Purpose: That children play a Bible game to reinforce the Bible concept of pleasing God and to encourage positive attitudes about doing things that please God.

Materials

☐ Three game boards (one for each of three players) made as follows:
   1. Use a felt pen to divide each game board (made from shirt cardboard or cardboard of similar size) into four equal sections.
   2. Put a different gummed seal in each section of the game board. Use gummed seals that depict such things as children praying, a family reading the Bible, child walking to church, a child doing a kind act. Seals of this type are published by Standard Publishing and can be purchased in Christian bookstores. (Other ideas: pictures from old Sunday School papers, hand-drawn pictures. Artistic parents or grandparents may want to help you create games like this one.)
☐ Sixteen game cards (four cards for each of the four pictures used on the game boards). Make cards as follows:
   1. Cut eight index cards in half to make 16 game cards.
   2. Put a gummed seal on each game card. Make four cards using each of the four pictures on the game board (for example, make four cards with a picture of a church, four cards of a child praying, etc.)

127

Procedure

1. Shuffle the cards and lay them face down.
2. Children take turns drawing a card, matching the picture on the card to the one on the board and covering it. If the picture is already covered, the child turns the card face down on the bottom of the pile.
3. The child who covers all four pictures first gets to tell one way he can please God.

Guided Conversation Ideas

"We'll take turns today playing this game. When you pick a card, think of how the picture shows someone pleasing God. Kim, what does your card show about pleasing God? How else can we please God? Why is God pleased when we come to church? Tell me something you do at home that pleases God. This card shows children praying. What do you think they are saying to God?"